AN ADVENTURE OF GREAT DIMENSION

The Launching of the
Chicago Assyrian Dictionary

TRANSACTIONS
of the
AMERICAN PHILOSOPHICAL SOCIETY
Held at Philadelphia
For Promoting Useful Knowledge
Volume 92   Pt. 3

AN ADVENTURE OF GREAT DIMENSION

The Launching of the
Chicago Assyrian Dictionary

ERICA REINER

American Philosophical Society
Philadelphia   •   2002

ISBN: 0-87169-923-0
US ISSN: 0065-9746

Library of Congress Cataloging-in-Publication Data

Reiner, Erica, 1926–
    An adventure of great dimension: the launching of the Chicago Assyrian dictionary / Erica Reiner
        p. cm. — (Transactions of the American Philosophical Society, ISSN 0065-9746 ; v. 92, pt 3
    Includes bibliographical references and index.
    ISBN 0-87169-923-0 (pbk.)
    1. Chicago Assyrian dictionary. 2. Akkadian language—Dictionaries—English. I. Title. II. Series

PJ3525 .R45 2002
492'.132—dc21
                                                                                2002028238

Design and Composition
Book Design Studio II

CONTENTS

FOREWORD

The great museums of the world had their origins in the "cabinets of curiosities" of seventeenth century princes, inducing the obeisance of courtiers and the wonderment of visiting peers at the power of a potentate to display what God wrought in such diversity. That and the Age of Enlightenment that followed were also an age in which exploration began in earnest. European travelers girdled the globe, long anticipating the routes that would one day be taken by the conquering fleets and armies of their countrymen. A delayed product of this time of far-ranging curiosity, long held back by the enormous intellectual difficulties of coming to grips with dead languages where there was no accidental discovery of a Rosetta Stone to unlock their meaning, was the discovery of two and more millennia of human achievement in Babylonia and Assyria that were previously known only as derivative wisps of memory and a scattering of kings and exploits filtered through alien interpreters into the books of the Old Testament.

Renaissance Europe had taken the Classical world to its bosom centuries earlier, but the discovery of far more remote antecedents was initially unsettling. Today, of course, the ancient Fertile Crescent joins several other early civilizations around the world into which we all recognize that the frontiers of scholarship have been pressing forward for more than a century. But what sets Babylonia and Assyria apart from the others is the vast corpus of records that scribes there unintentionally preserved for us through the medium of cuneiform writing on clay tablets.

No other ancient civilization left such a record. The literary corpus disappoints us through the rigidity of its constraints on innovation outside a confined stream of tradition, but the contents of that stream and a smaller, equally constrained set of historical chronicles nonetheless bring us face to face with what were for millennia the founding and legitimizing statements of a civilized, urban way of life. And alongside these genres, in spite of enormous gaps in sequence and distribution that make general patterns harder to identify, are economic and administrative documents, and for later periods letters, almost beyond reckoning as

to numbers and variety. For cultural historians and compara-
tivists, and for historically oriented social scientists of every
description, the subject matter of the field of Assyriology is an
unequaled prize.

My own attention turns first to material relics of human behav-
ior. Mute though they may be, at least they escape from the occu-
pational myopia of ancient scribes, who were dependent on elite
patronage and often ensnared in recapitulating changeless tradi-
tions. Archaeological evidence can serve in that sense as an
important complement to written records. And of course it is all we
have to work with for the millennia preceding writing. But only
exceptionally can it bring us close to the complex substance of real
human interactions, or the immediacy of human events of any
kind. At best, it tends to offer only ambiguous, undependable
indices of human agency. If we seek to detect meaning in a wholly
vanished and unfamiliar way of life, whether at the level of individuals or collectivities, it is to the extraordinary cuneiform record
that we must turn.

It is deeply to be regretted that very little documentation seems to
have survived from the early days of the Chicago Assyrian
Dictionary (hereafter "CAD"). Nothing is known to suggest that its
potential transdisciplinary significance was recognized, although
the commanding vision of his field held by the founder of the
Oriental Institute, James Henry Breasted, certainly introduces this
possibility. But as late as the middle of the last century, when efforts
finally turned to the actual production of a dictionary after decades
devoted to filling file-cases with short cuneiform passages illustrat-
ing words and their uses, Erica Reiner makes clear that there was at
first little recognition of the awesome complexity of the task. The
initially prevailing assumption was that meanings could fairly
quickly be extracted by scrutinizing these notes, and the task hand-
ily concluded in less than a decade. Now with this account we can
look back on a half-century and more of arduous labor by many
hands. Many times the number of volumes originally anticipated
are already in print, and the last ones are finally nearing publication. Clearly, what kind of dictionary was needed, and was possible,
somehow was transformed. Here is the absorbing account of the
crucial discussions and decisions—and, yes, confrontations—
through which that happened.

Not neglecting the remote and subsequent history of the undertaking, Reiner focuses particularly on the painful reformulation of
the task that took place during her early years of participation in it
in the 1950s and 1960s. This involved the fateful interaction of truly

eminent scholars holding clashing visions of how their field was to advance. For Thorkild Jacobsen a comprehensive dictionary was at best a distant, perhaps an unattainable, goal. The prior objective, at least, was penetration to the heart of a few key words and their conceptual underpinning, guided by immense personal knowledge of relevant sources and trained intuition. Meaning would flow outward to an ill-defined, essentially passive, wider community of scholars from the hands of the elect of Assyriology. Establishing consistent, overarching webs of ancient belief and thought was the primary objective of Assyriological scholarship. Within those webs, but of no immediate significance, derived particulars might or might not presently find their places. For Leo Oppenheim, and for Erica Reiner as his younger colleague and sharer of his basic outlook, the task instead was to make available the intelligible sum total of the written record to potential collaborators with many other interests, some already emergent but others still unforeseen. And that meant getting on with producing a dictionary capable of meeting this wide set of demands with all deliberate speed.

Benno Landsberger, an unrivaled, older magister of the field in the eyes of both Jacobsen and Oppenheim, in the end supported Oppenheim at every critical juncture. But his personal respect and sympathy for Jacobsen were also evident. A gigantic figure as he rightly emerges in these pages, he complained at times about the "insane haste" of the project. One can sense that he felt in his bones the bottomless well from which meanings could be drawn, and he was surely proud of his own pioneering role in having done so for decades. But in the end, also conscious that his was now a leading place in bringing the best of central European scholarship on antiquity to a new setting and set of demands on a new continent, he resolutely joined in Oppenheim's conviction that the project could not be allowed to tarry over some few, subjectively chosen words at the expense of so many others.

Oppenheim fortunately found an opportunity to put forward his comprehensive vision of the future of Assyriology. Almost a call to arms, his "Assyriology — Why and How?" deserves to be read as a companion to the present work. The battle for synthesis is the battle Assyriologists must fight, he decided, their "raison d'être, even though it is a battle that can have no victorious outcome." Acknowledging that the growing breadth and complexity of the field were tending to drive its members into overspecialization and "peripheral skirmishes," he saw its future in increasingly close cooperation with specialists in science, law, medicine, technology, and cultural anthropology. "The Assyriologist should become aware that he holds the keys to a potential wealth of information covering more than two millennia of one of the first great civilizations. If he is in need of a raison d'être, here it is." Something approaching omnidirectionality in its potential for communicating this wealth was the corollary of this stirring goal that he saw for the CAD. It could and would need further revision as time went on, since no formulations of meanings could ever be eternally satisfactory. But in the meantime, while organized around lists of words, it needed to become in substance something much more than a dictionary and almost closer to an encyclopedic introduction to a great civilization that would otherwise remain "dead."

Coming late in the day, as a newly appointed director of the Oriental Institute with a level of responsibility that required me to settle upon the CAD's leadership and thus decide the issue, I temporized for a time while consulting widely. But in the end I concurred warmly in the course that has finally made the CAD not only a reality of the kind Oppenheim envisioned but one of the great and enduring humanistic achievements of our time. As always, there were costs. Thorkild Jacobsen, who had done more than anyone to shape my own understanding of Mesopotamia as a graduate student barely a decade before, and under whose encouragement I had gone on to begin an ambitious program of field surveys in Iraq, shortly left Chicago altogether and took up a post at Harvard. Such is the consequential, central story of this absorbingly personal memoir on a momentous enterprise by its only surviving participant.

Robert McC. Adams

ACKNOWLEDGMENTS

To chronicle, as the last surviving witness, the trials and the satisfactions of launching the Chicago Assyrian Dictionary is a solitary task. I was fortunate to have had much support and encouragement throughout. Hence, to friends and colleagues who read and commented on various stages of the manuscript (S. C. Humphreys, H. Hunger, A. D. Kilmer, M. T. Larsen, D. E. Pingree, J. M. Renger, M. T. Roth) I am indebted for their criticisms and suggestions; to the Oriental Institute and especially its archivist John Larson for access to some of the documents used and quoted I am grateful; to the manuscript editor Peter T. Daniels who uncannily guessed right what I wanted to express I owe many of the felicities of expression. But my greatest debt is to Robert McC. Adams, who read various drafts in manuscript and urged me to expand and deepen this tale, and whose Preface puts it into a larger perspective.

Chicago, March 2002

INTRODUCTION

"Histories of such projects are best written after they are completed," So I said in 1980, in a lecture given at the University of Chicago. If I nevertheless attempt to write such a history, it is because the project is very close to completion and my association with it has loosened, as I am no longer editor in charge. It is also prudent to set down my experiences and memories before they disappear with me. The difficulty of such a task is evident. As one scholar put it:

> ... a large part of the more recent period falls within one's own period of scholarly life, so that one has become familiar with many of the relevant writings. However, even for that period, one is confronted, to one's surprise, with uncertainties and doubts about seemingly simple matters. To gauge the influence of one scholar upon another turns out to be a subtle task which only rarely can be fulfilled to one's own satisfaction. And at every step one becomes painfully aware that a linguist is not automatically also a historian or a psychologist.[1]

The situation easily applies to the present task, if we substitute "Assyriologist" for "linguist" in the previous sentence.

A history of the *Chicago Assyrian Dictionary* (CAD) is only a small part of the history of Assyriology, even of the Assyriology in the 20th century. Such histories have multiplied in the last decades of the past century as various disciplines have sought to understand and record the dynamics that brought them to their current plateau.[2]

Histories may take stock of where one stands in the flow of development of the discipline; they may express nostalgia for the past, seek to justify what has gone before, or strive to build a basis for what the historian would like to see emerge. Assyriology as a discipline has not yet found its historiographer. Its 19th-century origins were traced by Mogens T. Larsen but he chose to begin by bringing out first the history of explorers and excavators of the early days, and the excitement of discovering the remains of "The might that was Assyria"[3] in his *The Conquest of Assyria.*[4]

Beyond recording the history of the explorations of Mesopotamia or of the decipherment of cuneiform writing that has been described in many books, there remains a need for—in the words of an anthropologist—an appraisal of the discipline, and an investigation of its dynamics.[5]

The history of the Chicago Assyrian Dictionary Project can, I believe, contribute to the appraisal of Assyriology and illuminate some aspects of it as practiced in the second half of the 20th century. The project is nearly finished; the Dictionary almost completed. Its 21 volumes (in 2002, two in manuscript and two still in press) encompass the entire known vocabulary of the Akkadian (that is, Assyrian and Babylonian) language over its more than two-thousand-year-long history. But its value goes beyond translating Akkadian words into English. From an originally purely philological enterprise the CAD evolved into a sort of encyclopaedia that, in Oppenheim's words, "aims, on the semantic side, to relate meanings to the social context and the technological background in which the references occur, and strives toward a useful and revealing coordination of the Akkadian and the Sumerian evidence (which is essential for the semantic history of many words), and attempts to present each reference in a small but meaningful section of its context."[6] Through this approach its volumes recapture the cultural history of the Near East from c. 2500 B. C. to the first century A. D.

The Dictionary has also shaped the field through the continuous influx of collaborators from all over the world; it has attracted some of the best Assyriologists, so that the CAD contains a precipitate of the scholars who made major contributions to Assyriology in the 20th century.

"The CAD is the fulfillment of the dream of James H. Breasted, Egyptologist and ancient historian, the first Director of the Oriental Institute of the University of Chicago, and the man who initiated the CAD project in 1921 and was its guiding spirit until his death in 1935."[7] So wrote I. J. Gelb, the man responsible for the CAD's revival after World War II.

A dictionary of Egyptian began to appear in 1926; it was initiated in Berlin in 1897, during those closing years of the 19th century that also saw the birth of similar all-encompassing enterprises; I need mention here only the *OED* (1884–1928)[8] and the *Thesaurus Linguae Latinae*, begun in 1894. The newly founded Oriental Institute, under Breasted, was anxious to take its place on the stage of ancient Oriental studies. Possibly responding to the challenge of the Berlin Egyptologists, the Assyriologists at Chicago decided to compile an Assyrian Dictionary. Indeed, in his 1933 *The Oriental Institute*, it is the Oxford dictionary and the Egyptian dictionary that Breasted cites as models for an Assyrian dictionary.[9]

I doubt that any of the scholars at the Oriental Institute at that time—the Assyrian Dictionary's first editor, D. D. Luckenbill, or his successor, Edward Chiera—had the vaguest idea what the problems associated with such a project were, until Gelb, a junior Assyriologist, appeared on the scene in 1929. It was Chiera's untimely death in 1933 that catapulted Gelb into the forefront, and it was through him that the project landed on firmer footing. Even Gelb—young as he was at the time—could not foresee the difficulties inherent in such an enterprise as the CAD. He, too, believed, or perhaps only hoped, that once every reference to the word was collected, its meaning would become immediately evident and that collecting the material and organizing it in some logical and orderly way was at least halfway to capturing the meaning.

This incontestably major scholarly enterprise that is the now almost completed CAD may have arisen, ironically, from a wish to outdo the Germans or at least to prove to the world that America could hold its own against, and better, the simultaneously despised and envied Germans. It also is ironic that ultimately the viability of the CAD project was precisely due to post-World War II immigrants from Europe.

There were of course other circumstances that made an Assyrian Dictionary Project desirable. No dictionary of the Akkadian language, then mostly known as Assyrian or Assyro-Babylonian, had been compiled since Edwin Norris first attempted such a dictionary (1868–1872) that, however, remained unfinished. A monumental project was launched by Friedrich Delitzsch, the *Assyrisches Wörterbuch*, but he abandoned the grandiose enterprise after the publication of three fascicles (1887–1890) that did not even exhaust the words beginning with the first letter of the Semitic alphabet, aleph; instead he concentrated on a *Handwörterbuch* that appeared in 1896. At Johns Hopkins University in Baltimore, the scholar William Muss-Arnolt had prepared a "concise dictionary" that listed definitions in both English and German and included bibliographical references; the first of its two volumes appeared in 1905. In the 1930s in Germany Bruno Meissner had begun collecting material for a dictionary of Akkadian—a project that was interrupted by the war and brought to a temporary halt by the death of Meissner in 1947.

With Chiera's death in 1933, under Arno Poebel, a Sumerologist with little interest in Akkadian lexicography, the CAD project too sank into a state of suspended animation. It struggled to preserve its identity until and during World War II, when the protagonists were called to participate, in various capacities, in the war effort.

FIGURE 1. A set of the CAD (published volumes and volumes in proofs).

It is the CAD's re-emergence from slumber under Gelb and its subsequent fate, with which my own life and career became inextricably embroiled, that the following account deals with. It is a personal history, which takes its significance not from the narrator's life and person but from the extraordinary individuals who were the players and from the import of the project that they strove to complete, a project that was dubbed by one of its most important participants "an adventure of great dimension."[10]

THE SETTING

The *Chicago Assyrian Dictionary* (CAD) was an enterprise that modeled itself on the great thesauri planned and initiated at the end of the 19th century and the beginning of the next century, of which the *Oxford English Dictionary* (OED) is the best known and possibly the most outstanding example. The CAD itself was to follow the model of the Egyptian dictionary prepared in Berlin,[11] and it was undertaken in this spirit and administered with this aim. It was to stand beside the great historical or etymological dictionaries of the era such as the *Littré*, the *Thesaurus Linguae Latinae*, and the historical and dialect dictionaries en vogue.

But the CAD had another purpose, one that was to become increasingly dominant as it underwent numerous reorganizations. This purpose was never stated in the dictionary itself; however, as the CAD progressed it encompassed more and more of the context of the words studied, a context not solely, and not even predominantly, in syntactic terms but in cultural and semantic terms. These contexts reflected the interests of the writers and editors, interests that happened to be widely diverging and thus collectively covering a wide spectrum of the ancient Mesopotamian world. Thus, the CAD became a tool for recapturing an ancient civilization, and for studying its social and economic structure, its material culture, its values, and its beliefs, in short, it became a vehicle using an anthropological approach to understand and explicate a civilization alien and remote in time or, as A. Leo Oppenheim preferred to put it, a "dead" civilization.[12]

Oppenheim—who was the moving force of the enterprise from 1954 onward and who was supported in his striving for its survival and publication by his senior colleague Benno Landsberger and by me, then a junior Assyriologist—was well aware of this distinctiveness of the CAD. "In collaboration with Professor Landsberger and Erica Reiner we have succeeded in showing new ways and methods in Akkadian lexicography, as has now been tellingly proven by the Handwörterbuch of von Soden that has put in relief our own contribution."[13]

Forging tools happens in the heat of the forge, in a heat that may also singe and destroy. The heat in which the tool that became the CAD was forged was no exception. As time went by, this tool was further honed by all who wished to use it, and it still remains in need of further work and effort. It is this process that I aim to evoke.

The CAD grew up in the atmosphere of the venerable humanistic disciplines attempting to define themselves. Assyriology, like other philological disciplines, was well ensconced among the comparable disciplines of classical philology and Old Testament theology; its antiquarian interests were inherited from 19th-century concerns.

In the United States, the postwar era was a period of reassessment of the past and of large-scale enterprises in the historical and social disciplines. At the University of Chicago alone, such symposia as the Darwin Centennial[14] in 1959 and City Invincible[15]—the latter at the Oriental Institute, at the suggestion of Robert J. Braidwood, Gustave E. von Grunebaum, and John A. Wilson and organized by a committee that also included Thorkild Jacobsen and Carl Kraeling—in 1958 sought to expand the anthropological horizon by making appeal to history, political science, and, in the case of Darwin, to the natural sciences as well. Here was founded and edited for many decades the journal *Current Anthropology*, with the innovative format of discussions and comments following the main article, devised, as was the Darwin Centennial, by the anthropologist Sol Tax. Of course, to some European scholars transplanted to the United States, such symposia seemed a weird American invention:

> The "City Invincible" makes good bedtime reading. It informs about this country's mentality. One of the achievements of Kraeling, the director who has since resigned, was the so-called symposium and this book; the two cost several tens of thousands of dollars. The money was provided by Rockefeller, who thus created a pendant to the "urbanization" project of the late anthropologist Redfield (often cited in the O.I.). The latter had received a subvention of about a hundred thousand from Ford. On the other hand, it is impossible to raise any money to print a non-popular book.[16]

These comments notwithstanding, Landsberger participated with great gusto in the symposium, introducing a discussion on scribal education and basking in the attention devoted to him.

It was inevitable that the CAD, under the direction of this forward-looking generation, would participate in the reassessment and renewal of the philological sciences. "Often, indeed almost always, our lexicography is cultural history in disguise, even if no one will go as far as Jacobsen, to wit, to write an entire book (which I consider despite a bitter feud about it, valuable) about awīlum ['man']."[17] Once the project was proven feasible, and once it did go forward, it became a magnet for Assyriologists for many years. Colleagues in the United States and abroad wanted to take part by sending—without remuneration—words excerpted from unpublished texts, and often transliterations and translations of such unpublished texts themselves; they contributed not only material, but also manpower, by encouraging young scholars to go to Chicago and help the CAD, and in the process receive a training unmatched elsewhere.[18]

While a "short" dictionary (Handwörterbuch) was compiled in Germany by a single mature scholar with the help of successive assistants, the CAD has always been a true collective enterprise, with its senior editors arguing about the meanings of the words and the organization of their presentation. In a sense the results were often only prolegomena to a dictionary, or rather a tool for future efforts to determine the words' meanings. Landsberger acknowledged this in a letter to his friend and disciple Fritz Rudolf Kraus:

> Anyone who reads your speech [i. e., the draft of Kraus's inaugural lecture at the University of Leiden] must receive the impression that the future lexicon will contain the meanings of the Akkadian words. However, in most cases determining them is beyond our powers; true, if I were to work on it very intensively, perhaps a few meanings would come out. Leaving aside obscure plant names and the like, I can state that the meanings of 60% of the Akkadian words are unknown and that it is not even the aim of the Dictionary to establish them. If Gelb were again to obtain the exclusive directorship and find slaves for it, the Dictionary would turn into a mere (and bad!) word list. Less so with us, Landsberger and Oppenheim, more so without us, Landsberger and Oppenheim, the Dictionary becomes only a means handed to the next generation for finding the meanings."[19]

This stated, Landsberger wrestled with establishing the meanings of complex sociocultural terms, while not abandoning his interest in the native terms of grammatical function (modal adverbs, and the like) or of material culture. He was more stubborn than Oppenheim in delving into the vocables that interested him, and at the same time trying to be more faithful to the original than Oppenheim, whose inclination was to "modernize" the translations.[20]

This striving for balance among the CAD staff between, as Landsberger expressed the dilemma, "maximality" and "minimality," pervaded the history of the project. Outside Chicago, minimality was espoused in 1999 in a 450-page "concise" dictionary that has successfully done away with all the niceties and the reservations of both the CAD and von Soden's *Handwörterbuch*.[21]

On the positive side, two other dictionaries of ancient languages, one, of Hittite, at the University of Chicago, and the other, of

Sumerian, at the University of Pennsylvania, both claim to follow the example of the CAD in layout and style as well as philosophy, as stated in their respective Forewords.[22] Comparisons should not be made since these two dictionaries had—and will have—to fight their own separate battles, both at home and in the wider scholarly world. The *Chicago Assyrian Dictionary* wishes them well in their long journey toward their still far-away completion. More pertinent is a comparison with the University of Michigan's *Middle English Dictionary*, that figures rather prominently in this history of the CAD.

DRAMATIS PERSONAE

The major players in the development of the Assyrian Dictionary were I. J. Gelb, Thorkild Jacobsen, Benno Landsberger, and A. Leo Oppenheim. The first two were instrumental in relaunching the project after World War II, and their role will be discussed again and again. But it was the last two who stayed with it until the project had become a viable enterprise, and it is proper that their scholarly life and contribution to Assyriology be briefly sketched here.

Landsberger and Oppenheim each proclaimed a credo; more important, these proclamations continue to be evoked whenever their stance on Assyriology is appraised. For Benno Landsberger, it is his famous *Eigenbegrifflichkeit* (the singularity [of the Babylonian world]), which he himself characterized as a "programmatical essay";[23] for Leo Oppenheim, *Assyriology—why and how?* Their two manifestos may appear, at least on the surface, diametrically opposite. Landsberger proclaimed the special, unique character of Babylonian language and culture in his inaugural lecture (*Antrittsvorlesung*) at the University of Leipzig in 1926 (published in *Islamica*, volume 2, in 1926); thirty years later Oppenheim insisted, in the first volume (1956) of the new journal *Current Anthropology*, that Assyriology will remain a dead field unless it opens itself to the currents of modern science: anthropology, history of science, history of ideas, and the like.

LANDSBERGER

Landsberger's influence on the field is the most difficult to assess; he was a larger-than-life figure, the hero of countless funny stories and anecdotes, the circulation of which he carefully encouraged. Anecdotes often, and in particular with Landsberger, are an expression of admiration and affection—and Landsberger himself was a great purveyor and cultivator of anecdotes about himself. But anecdotes also draw down to our own level a figure who seems to loom too high, by exposing his or her foibles.

A simple way of defining Landsberger's influence on Assyriology would be to list his students and disciples, beginning with Adam Falkenstein, Wolfram von Soden, Hans Gustav Güterbock, Lubor Matouš, and Fritz Rudolf Kraus, who themselves shaped, often by perpetuating Landsberger's values, the field. And then there were those disciples whose works Landsberger himself claimed (not very generously) as his own, from the book on the *Akkadische Namengebung* of J. J. Stamm (1939) to the article "A Faithful Lover" by Moshe Held (1961). Since 1931 he also exercised his influence as editor of the *Zeitschrift für Assyriologie*, the most influential organ of Assyriology. The Neue Folge—new series—of the Leipziger Semitistische Studien (LSS) is headed by the dissertations of students of Landsberger.[24] The LSS list itself is distinguished by, of course, Landsberger's own *Kultischer Kalender*,[25] which has only in the past few years been partly superseded[26] and Part II of which, promised by Landsberger, never materialized. To do Assyriology was for Landsberger part of a learned gentleman's privilege, if not duty; he once said to the then young Assyriologist Paul Garelli, who passed this remark on to me, "Every educated person knows Akkadian, just as he does Greek or Latin."

Landsberger had produced practically no book of a general nature, at least not under his own name. Those of his works that were published as monographs in reality are extended articles.[27] Of course one could say that some of his articles are in reality small monographs.[28] Of *Samʿal* he himself said, "My review of Bossert has turned into a book."[29] Not that he lacked the ideas or the breadth for undertaking a major work. On the contrary: He started out on a topic, labeling the first section of his study Roman I, its first subsection capital A, which in turn began with Arabic 1, lower case a, and finally alpha. While he usually reached beta, and perhaps even b, the grandiose organization requiring B, 2, etc., not to speak of Roman II, never materialized. Rather, one idea led to the next, until eventually the ground plan of the edifice was forgotten. His articles were so dense, so chockful with asides and insights of detail, that it was impossible to file all the information in them. He was especially challenged by others' opinions and results. His most interesting work was written *against* someone. This need for the foil of the opinion of others may have been one of the reasons for his daily sessions with Jacobsen at the Oriental Institute, during which they discussed Sumerian grammar and sundry other topics.

A special mention must be made, of course, of the ten-odd volumes of the *Materials for the Sumerian Lexicon* (MSL), which represent a particular interest and accomplishment of Landsberger's. Begun in Leipzig, on commission from the Assyrian Dictionary Project, they also served as an excuse for the investigation of the meaning of families of words, an interest that also characterized the lexicography of the post-World War I age. Of course Landsberger could not have been unaffected by the intellectual currents of his age, and to these belonged the *Wörter und Sachen* ("words and their referents") approach then fashionable, which considers both form and meaning of the words with special concern for cultural facts. Outside the studies inspired by, and usually included in, the MSL volumes, his 1926 study on the terms for "early" and "late" also testifies to this interest.[30] For the studies of material objects he liked to use technical books—well, not too technical—such as on the fauna, flora, and fish of Iraq, or Löw's *Flora*,[31] but he especially favored Meyer's *Konversationslexicon*, which was proudly displayed in his office.

Landsberger's interest in grammar and linguistics, evident already in his lecture on singularity (*Eigenbegrifflichkeit*), lasted well into his later years. In Chicago he still gave classes, albeit unofficial ones after his retirement, on Semitic linguistics; indeed, he was inordinately proud that he knew about Noam Chomsky and that a student of his was applying this newfangled linguistic aproach to Sumerian.[32] He discussed many features of Semitic and Akkadian with the late Haiim Rosén, a linguist from the Hebrew University in Jerusalem, who audited his classes in Chicago. Rosén used to say that Landsberger was his informant. He used Landsberger as he would have used a native speaker, testing on him phrases and idioms to see whether they were acceptable; Landsberger could always be trusted to respond, "You can say that" or "You cannot say that." While Landsberger agreed to serve as informant, he could not countenance that anyone make up an Akkadian sentence to use as an example. This simply was not allowed. Many of Landsberger's innovations in the grammar of Akkadian, such as the "Landsbergersche Tempuslehre," were professed in classes only; eventually they were incorporated by his former student von Soden in his unrivaled and sole authoritative grammar of Akkadian.[33]

It is Landsberger's collaboration with Paul Koschaker that opened the field of legal history for Assyriologists. Whereas a few previous Assyriologists had enlisted the advice and collaboration of jurists, for example, Felix Peiser and Arthur Ungnad had collaborated with Josef Kohler, Landsberger's collaboration with Koschaker was more of a symbiosis. In Leipzig, the two shared a seminar room, a library, and of course students. They jointly gave classes in which one analyzed the language, the other the legal implications—and the "one" and the "other" often interchanged. Koschaker himself learned enough Akkadian to participate meaningfully in the discussion; perhaps the fact that the recently uncovered Nuzi archives were written in a barbarized Akkadian made his task a bit easier.

Similarly, Landsberger enlisted the advice of I. Krumbiegel for his *Fauna*.[34] To the very end he sought to enrich his understanding by reaching out to friends and colleagues in various fields: Benedict Einarsson of the Department of Classics for Greek, his physician Dr. Isaiah I. Ritter, and Edith Ritter who became interested in Akkadian medical texts, for medical lore. His last project, a book that remained unfinished, was basically a retrospective in which he took up the various motifs of the field that had occupied him: history of law, Near Eastern society, and again *Eigenbegrifflichkeit…*

The CAD owes more to Benno Landsberger than is apparent. In addition to safeguarding the future of the project by giving testimony to its quality and worth, he studied extensively and in depth a great number of words and word families. Landsberger's insights and analyses of words written well after his passing can still benefit the project, as in the case of the adverb tūša that he studied in connection with other modal particles for volume M of the CAD and that proved useful to the editors of volume T. If the CAD staff ever had a quarrel with Landsberger, it was on account of his in-depth and consequently long-lasting study of the lemma (dictionary entry). Many entries were subjected to what he called "liebevolle Versenkung"; it usually involved re-examining the cuneiform, preferably the original, but at least a photo, lining up synonyms and antonyms, and probing the Sumerian background of the word or the concept.

Landsberger's insights were eagerly sought; some former students submitted everything they wrote to him. In fact, he needed disciples—*famuli*—around him. Long after his retirement he gave unofficial classes in Sumerian, after a good dinner at the private home of Dr. Ritter, to assorted University of Chicago students. A great number of students in turn served as Landsberger's assistants or secretaries, and those who had no official title clustered around him as "Privatschüler." We junior members of the staff were happy if he required our help with finding the appropriate files or even a mislaid pencil or pen; there was always something to learn from him.

Landsberger also played a large role in the life of the project. This was stressed by Oppenheim, who stated that

[Landsberger] contributed decisively in helping to create the intellectual atmosphere characteristic of the "Third Floor" of the Oriental Institute, where the CAD took root and found its own identity. But on this I would rather quote a few sentences from an unpublished paper entitled "Progress in Assyriology" given by Benno Landsberger at the General Session of the Annual Meeting of the American Oriental Society on April 14, 1965:

> I am not indulging in trivialities when I point out that even if all the meanings of the words are wrong, the dictionaries maintain their value as word collections. Nor am I indulging in generalities when I state that between complete misunderstanding and raw understanding there are stages in which you partially hit the mark; but between external understanding and what is called penetration there is an ascending scale of degrees of comprehension, until you reach the *Eigenbegrifflichkeit*, and have the happy feeling that the sentence or even the word is the microcosmos that reflects the macrocosmos of this over-rich culture, with its permanence and change.
>
> Let me describe a few experiences that I have had with the project—this time, the CAD, which is still called a project although more justly it could be called an antiproject, since it differs from other projects still to be mentioned; it differs in this way: it does not postpone the final action indefinitely or leave decision for the next generation; it ignores almost frivolously[35] both systematization and specialization; it is neither deterred nor frustrated. In short, it is an adventure of great dimension, with both the dangers and the unexpected findings of an adventure…Any user of the CAD must be tolerant both of anticipation and of self-correction. As our lexicographical techniques advance, the detrimental effects of isolating words from their semantic families will be progressively avoided.[36]

FIGURE 2. At the Ritters (Edith Ritter, Landsberger, Güterbock).

OPPENHEIM

It is difficult to imagine for today's Assyriologist, who is accustomed to wielding the intellectual tools of anthropology, sociology, economic history, that these fields were closed to Assyriologists and might have remained inaccessible had it not been for A. Leo Oppenheim. It was he who forcefully, one might say brutally, challenged the field of Assyriology in his programmatic essay "Assyriology—Why and How?" that appeared in the then new journal, *Current Anthropology*. It was reprinted in his *Ancient Mesopotamia*, a book that included such scandalously titled chapters as "Why a 'Mesopotamian religion' should not be written." Those of his readers who never got beyond the title of the chapter accused him of being "antireligion," "nihilistic," and the like. Few bothered to examine his arguments. But the novelty in Oppenheim's approach was that he looked at the field with the eyes of an anthropologist: "I am a cultural anthropologist who happens to work with a civilization whose records are in a dead language and a strange script" was the way he liked to define himself. When faced with economic history, he looked at Mesopotamia from the perspective of an economic historian, and indeed trained himself for that role by attending for several years the monthly seminar led by Karl Polányi at Columbia University in New York City.

While Oppenheim enjoyed writing articles that were based on, or included considerations of, current theories, his articles had their origins not in abstract theory but in texts. One must not forget his editions of texts: the Dream-book, the Glass texts, the Reports of the Astrologers that Hermann Hunger brought to completion,[37] and the Neo-Babylonian texts eventually published as CT 55, 56, and 57. The latter he had analyzed and excerpted and even had pasted up for publication in a topical organization according to their content, but he did not live to set down and publish their significance for the Neo-Babylonian temple economy.[38] He used to say that he had to renew his strength, like Antaeus returning to the earth, by returning to the texts themselves.

With each new book, he annexed—or rather opened up to the Orientalist—yet another intellectual domain. With the Dream-book, it was psychology; with his study on Beer and Brewing, but especially the Glass book, it was technology, a subject that intrigued him from early days, and to which he contributed, although not in published form, in his study of the Material Culture in the Neo-Babylonian period. Medicine was as intriguing to him as Conchology. As he prepared to study the astrological reports, he did not so much expect to cover the history of astrono-my—a subject he was content to leave to David Pingree, for whose appointment at the Oriental Institute of the University of Chicago he was responsible—as to investigate the careers of the intellectu-als in Mesopotamia. The role and status of the scribes was the sub-ject he broached at the Venice symposium organized by *Daedalus*, the proceedings of which were not published until 1975,[39] and which he further expanded in the lectures (*leçons*) he gave at the Collège de France in 1971.

Before Denise Schmandt-Besserat had developed her thesis on counters as precursors of writing, even before the clay bullae con-taining such counters had been identified, Oppenheim gave the evidence for the use of such counters in the administration of herds in his article on an "Operational Device" published in 1959.[40] In many areas his papers were pathbreakers: Oppenheim's inclina-tion was to open up new perspectives and new fields and methods of research, leaving to others the opportunity of expanding them, not to close doors to the young and their new ideas.

He approached the field from an outside perspective. In Chicago, he made friends with anthropologists (Sydney Slotkin and Sol Tax) and was stimulated by their interests, and they made available to him a forum that he needed. He was an avid reader of books dealing with both intellectual and material culture. He would have made a good architect, and his draftsmanship became evident as he was editing words for the CAD in which the inserts and transfers showed a clean and sure hand—that was, of course, before the word processor made it easy to discard earlier versions that had contained sometimes irretrievable ideas and formulations.

He gave of himself with total dedication, and also demanded the same from his students and collaborators. His working style served as example, quite intentionally so. He joined the group of scholars who maintained that you can only teach by example, as did Michael Polányi. His aim was to emulate other fields of scholar-ship, such as the Classics; he wished that quotes from Akkadian and Sumerian need not be translated, as Latin and Greek quotes were not needed to be translated, at least there was such a time not long ago. He did not look down on the Mesopotamians as some sort of primitive, barbaric people; nor did he accept that a text in Akkadian was something exotic, to be italicized or translated; he thought that this would be unheard of for a text in Greek.

Oppenheim created, by introducing new terminology, a frame-work that has continued to serve new generations of scholars; it comes so naturally to us that we no longer associate with

Oppenheim the phrases "the great organizations" and "the stream of tradition." To quote the Foreword to the "Festfiche" that was presented to him on the occasion of his 70th birthday: "Current approaches to Assyriology have been decisively shaped by the work of Leo Oppenheim. ... Texts for him are only means to understand cultural history, and he has thus greatly helped to establish Assyriology as a discipline of the cultural sciences." The liberating effect of his example facilitated the work of members of a younger generation.

Yet I believe that the Chicago Assyrian Dictionary will be regarded, in spite of other editors who succeeded him, as Oppenheim's major lasting contribution. He himself so considered it, saying often "scripta volant " (the written word vanishes), a travesty of the saying "verba volant, scripta manent" (the spoken word vanishes, the written word endures). He was the person responsible for deciding on publication, and he tirelessly worked on word after word, volume after volume, in what Landsberger called "insane haste" to bring the CAD to a stage where it would be unthinkable that its progress be stopped. Indeed, Landsberger himself, in spite of his grumbling about the "insane haste" was instrumental in securing for the CAD the respect and the lease on life that its critics had tried to deny it.

Whenever Landsberger realized that he was wrong in some interpretation he had imposed on the CAD, he used to stick his head in at Oppenheim's door opening and say sotto voce: "I publicly apologize..." The intellectual honesty by which these scholars lived and functioned, acknowledging, publicly or not, that they could err and that it is not their own stature but the advancement of scholarship that is of vital importance, has given a particular distinction to the past century of Assyriology.

THE ASSYRIAN DICTIONARY
PROJECT

There exist several descriptions of the Chicago Assyrian Dictionary Project, but so far no account of its history has been attempted. Nor do Forewords to individual CAD volumes look back on any of the earlier ones; only the Introduction by I. J. Gelb to volume 1 (A) part 1, published in 1964 and the eighth in sequence of the CAD, contains a brief history of the project, and it was written mainly to acknowledge the contributions of the numerous collaborators.

Gelb's history adequately describes the plans and vicissitudes that the project had gone through since its inception in 1921. My aim is not to bring his report up to date and record the step-by-step evolution and growth of the project, but to recount the intellectual forces that shaped it; stated simply, to pinpoint what the catalyst was that made of the Assyrian Dictionary Project the *Chicago Assyrian Dictionary*.

To put it succinctly, as I had occasion to do in 1975:

> "The Assyrian Dictionary Project was conceived by distinguished scholars of a previous generation. It was fostered by the Dictionary Staff at the Oriental Institute and a continuous flow of young scholars. It was generously supported, financially and morally, by the directors of the Institute and the provosts of the University. It became the Chicago Assyrian Dictionary with Leo Oppenheim."[41]

My tale could begin in 1954 when, on a sunny spring day, Leo Oppenheim, at whose Michigan summer home I spent the weekend, decided to drive to Ann Arbor to visit the University of Michigan's Middle English Dictionary (MED) Project, and took me along. Oppenheim wanted to benefit from the experience of that project, that had only recently started publication. The editor, Sherman Kuhn, very kindly took us on a tour to see the workings of the project and, what was even more important, was very matter of fact about its inevitable shortcomings and problems.

"What happens when you find that you have forgotten a citation, omitted a word?" asked Oppenheim.

"We make a slip and put it in the files," he replied.

"And if you make a mistake?"

"It will be corrected in a volume of Additions and Corrections."
"Why did you start with the letter E?"
"It happened to be ready first."

Indeed, the Prefatory Note to volume III (1952) of the MED states: "For special reasons, E and F will be published first. They will be followed by D, C, B, A, in that order, whereupon G and the remaining letters will appear in alphabetic sequence." Sure enough, the Foreword to volume 6 (H) of the *Assyrian Dictionary*, dated 1956, starts with: "The publication of this dictionary...begins, for special reasons, with the letter H (Volume 6)." This statement in the Foreword is only a small token of the impact that the MED's style and schedule had on us. The visit to its headquarters was a major factor in the decision to go ahead and start publication of the Assyrian Dictionary.

But perhaps one ought to start the history of the Assyrian Dictionary in 1932, with the letter that Edward Chiera, director of the Assyrian Dictionary Project, wrote to the collaborators:

> Dear co-worker:
>
> It is no secret to you that at present we are making slight headway in the work for the Dictionary.... At the present rate of speed it would take us twenty-five years to complete the filing of the cards. Considering that, when the cards are all in, we have done only one-third of the work for the Dictionary, we would have to face the situation that the Dictionary will never be completed within the lifetime of any of us... [W]e have not kept constantly before our eyes the project as a whole and have concentrated too much on its individual parts.... Having lost sight of the project as a whole, we have attempted to attain perfection in the correction of the single manuscripts [i.e., manuscripts of Akkadian texts to be put in the files], when we should have known that perfection can never be attained.... No doubt we all agree that the Dictionary must be completed within a reasonably short time. As it is, whatever we do, I do not think ten years will suffice. And we do not have much more time than that even if we have that much. You all know that this project has been announced over ten years ago. When I was in Germany in 1928, I found there that my German colleagues were already making fun of a Dictionary that took so long in appearing....[42]

Unfortunately, little of the early material has been spared by the general housecleaning undertaken, during Carl Kraeling's directorship, by the executive secretary of the Oriental Institute, Margaret Fairbank Bell (later Margaret Bell Cameron). Chiera's letter was passed on to me by Margaret, who thought I might be interested in this piece of history. At the time I was very much involved in the Dictionary Project, and so, to a certain extent, was my friend Margaret, who had volunteered to read the dictionary articles for accuracy and felicity of English style. After her marriage in 1955 to George Cameron, professor of ancient history and Assyriology at

FIGURE 3. The Dictionary Room in the 1930s.

the University of Michigan, Margaret continued to take interest in the fate of the CAD and was a very generous supporter of it for many years. So, in the end Ann Arbor not only served as an impetus and a model through its *Middle English Dictionary*; it continued to extend its patronage over the CAD through the generosity of Mrs. Cameron.

The Dictionary languished between 1932, when Chiera was so concerned about its lack of progress, and its revival after World War II. I have no material for its history during that period. Our only source for the prewar period is I. J. Gelb's report, based on his own files from 1929 on.

In fact, it was at the initiative of Gelb, known as Jay to friends and colleagues, that new life was infused into the Dictionary after the war. Credit for the rebirth of the project after World War II and for securing the necessary financial support goes to him. Gelb was appointed editor-in-charge in 1947, after serving a year as acting editor. He had a tremendous energy that he channeled into the reorganizaton of the CAD. He convinced the University of Chicago's administration that the compilation and publication of the dictionary was feasible. He was fortunate in his appeal in that the dean of humanities was his colleague, the eminent Sumerologist Thorkild Jacobsen, who had served previously (from Dec. 1, 1946, to January 31, 1950) as director of the Oriental Institute.

Gelb's plan,[43] published in 1949, for the CAD to be finished in ten years (1947–1957) was divided into two phases. During the first five years, the files were to be completed; the second phase, the writing of articles, was to begin in 1952. The progress up to 1952 was reported by Gelb in 1952.[44] He had by that time attracted to Chicago Landsberger (1948) and Oppenheim (1947); and he continued to charge a number of nonresident scholars with preparing transliterations of various texts, sometimes with translations. These texts were then mimeographed, put on file cards, and filed by secretaries. He brought visiting research associates to the Oriental Institute to collect and process references for the CAD, and from there they usually went on to take up university posts in the United States or in their home countries. In 1952 he recruited two junior Assyriologists: Michael B. Rowton and me, for the resident staff.

These junior appointments were meant to replace those resident scholars who had died or retired: Samuel I. Feigin (d. 1950), Frederick W. Geers (retired 1950), as well as Alexander Heidel, whose research interests veered more and more toward Old Testament studies.

Gelb also devised the format for future dictionary entries. The CAD articles—the lemmata—were to be organized according to a scheme that he named Standard Operating Procedure (SOP), a procedure familiar to him from his career in the military and, he thought, applicable to the CAD. (For a detailed discussion of the SOP see the next chapter.)

It is not impossible that Gelb's scheme would have worked under different circumstances, with a different crew. It could not work with the highly individualistic staff of the CAD. Moreover, the schedule envisaged by Gelb in 1947—five years of writing followed by five years of publishing—was unrealistic, although no more or no less unrealistic than the plans and schedules of similar large-scale enterprises. Gelb's insistence on having a complete manuscript ready before beginning publication, while conceivable as long as the ten-year-plan seemed operational, became frustrating for the staff and threatened the very future of the CAD. In the end, Gelb's plan, Gelb's schedule, and perforce Gelb's layout of the dictionary article were of necessity abandoned, and survive now only in such stray vestiges as the occasional use by the staff of "lemma" for keyword, and some skeletal structure in the organization of a dictionary article reminiscent of the structure laid out in the SOP.

Still, the CAD might not have come into existence without Gelb's initiative and organizational ability, as was duly acknowledged by

Oppenheim in the Foreword of the first volume of the CAD to appear, Volume 6 (H).[45] One wonders, therefore, how this productive and enthusiastic scholar could have misjudged to such an extent the problems connected with the CAD. While his motto was *Citius emergit veritas ex errore quam e confusione* (Truth emerges more rapidly from error than from confusion),[46] when push came to shove he found himself unable to countenance error. True, Gelb's interests lay more in the theoretical questions of lexicography and lexicology than in practical questions of dictionary-making. The latter he considered "a rather dry and rewardless undertaking," to which scholars "should not be asked to sacrifice more of their time and interest."[47]

Another factor in the postwar history of the CAD was its relationship to a similar dictionary project based in Germany. When the academies of Heidelberg, Göttingen, Munich, and Berlin in Germany contemplated reviving the Assyrian dictionary begun by Meissner (1868–1947), Gelb, on a tour of Europe in the summer of 1950, entered into an agreement with Assyriologists in Germany, Vienna, and Rome at the congress of the German Oriental Society held at Marburg, Germany, in August 1950 "to coordinate the American and German Akkadian dictionary undertakings."[48] This so-called "Marburg agreement" was approved by the Union Académique Internationale in 1951.[49] It was discussed at a meeting of the CAD staff on October 4, 1950. As a result, reported Gelb:

> the German and American Akkadian Dictionary projects are linked together into one international undertaking, the results of which should be published in about six years in the form of one large dictionary prepared by the Chicago staff and one smaller school dictionary written by the German scholars.[50]

The Marburg agreement of 1950 and the arrival in Chicago of Oppenheim (1947) and Landsberger (1948) fell into the first five-year period as envisaged by Gelb's reorganization project. Landsberger was invited by Gelb specifically to work on the edition of the lexical texts, that is, the Sumerian and Akkadian bilingual vocabularies, for which he had been recruited earlier as a nonresident collaborator. He was appointed full professor with a salary of $8,000 a year in 1949.

The appointment of Landsberger was followed in 1949 by that of Hans Gustav Güterbock, the most distinguished Hittitologist of his generation, who had begun his studies with Landsberger in Leipzig and followed him to occupy the chair of Hittitology in Ankara in 1936. Although never officially a member of the CAD staff, Güterbock contributed to the quality of the project, indirectly by helping to interpret material from Hittite texts, but often more directly in the reading of texts from Mesopotamia, as he was famous for being able to read poorly preserved cuneiform signs from photographs, a talent to which Landsberger often had recourse. Güterbock's level-headed judgment was often sought by Landsberger in policy matters too. The intellectual and personal integrity of Güterbock earned him the respect of all his colleagues and students.

It seems, at least in retrospect, that a crucial factor in the eventual viability of the CAD was a coincidental age differential of about twenty years: Oppenheim was Landsberger's junior by fifteen years, and with my own appointment a younger scholar, twenty years younger than Oppenheim, came on the scene. In a pivotal position between the "grand old man" of the field and the energetic and willing young recruit, Oppenheim could count on wisdom and experience on the one hand, and on dedication and enthusiasm on the other. This knowledge may have helped him to persevere in the face of the various and sometimes traumatic fights that the project underwent in the years 1955–1962.

There was an affinity between the two senior scholars, in spite of the age difference, and it was manifested not only as congeniality in scholarship, but also on a personal level as Landsberger's letters to Kraus testify: "Oppenheim, by the way, is a good-natured fellow who does not take himself and his sloppiness too seriously. His knowledge of Assyriology is immense. He immediately offered to help me deal with practical matters and performs splendidly."[51] "He is a man of touching good nature, never misses a class of mine, and seems, according to the general opinion, to have radically improved in his recent publications."[52]

A possible reason for this affinity, which eventually extended to me too, may lie in our shared Central European background—what could be called the Austro-Hungarian connection.

To judge from his correspondence with his friend and former student Fritz Rudolf Kraus, Landsberger initially viewed the CAD project with skepticism. In October 1949 he wrote, "Even though I am convinced that with the present composition of the lexicographic staff the Dictionary can appear only as a debased Bezold, I have to avail myself of this opportunity ... The real Akkadian lexicon will naturally be published by von Soden."[53] Landsberger's allusion is to the *Babylonisch-assyrisches Glossar* compiled by the German Assyriologist Carl Bezold and prepared for publication by Albrecht Goetze. Published in 1926, it is a dictionary with few quotes and no references, with many incorrect entries. "This manual is of such a low standard that its use has been absolutely forbidden for all students for whose education I have been responsible"—thus a footnote of Landsberger's written in 1954.

Many Assyriologists had their "Bezold" interleaved, adding references and new attestations. Oppenheim's copy was already in tatters when I came to Chicago; when Mrs. Oppenheim urged him to have it rebound, he answered, "There is no need, I am writing a new one for myself."[54] The second author mentioned in Landsberger's letter, Wolfram von Soden, a former student of Landsberger's, is the scholar who was to take over the legacy of Meissner and produce the *Akkadisches Handwörterbuch*, finished in 1981, as Landsberger so uncannily predicted.

In spite of these misgivings and of his periodic complaints to Kraus of the pressure of the work, Landsberger enjoyed his Chicago tenure as he had every reason to. It was a safe haven after his years of exile in Turkey, where he was professor of Assyriology at Ankara University, having been dismissed from Leipzig by the Nazi regime in 1935; he had a chair that he was able to hold until his death in 1968, beyond retirement age (he turned 65 in 1955), funded in part by the Guggenheim Foundation; he also found congenial colleagues and devoted disciples. Landsberger also was allotted a research assistant: some served him part time but others full time; among them were W. W. Hallo, R. F. G. Sweet, Anne Draffkorn Kilmer, and Miguel Civil, all of whom eventually occupied chairs of Assyriology. His appointment was extended, year after year, at the request of the director of the Oriental Institute, on the basis of Landsberger's contributions:

> His work on the Assyrian Dictionary is of the greatest possible value to Dr. Oppenheim in connection with the publication of the successive volumes of the Dictionary (two volumes have now appeared), and his participation must be assured as long as he is able to carry the load. His standing as the world's greatest living authority in the Assyriological field guarantees for the Dictionary its high quality and is in no small measure involved in the acclaim with which it has been received in the scholarly world.[55]

After retirement Landsberger continued to work with students privately, students who were beyond their university years but continued to sit at his feet: the Arabist A. Motzkin; Moshe Held, who became professor at Columbia University, New York; and Mrs. Edith Ritter, the wife of his physician, who was interested in Babylonian medicine. It was a heavy burden on him to take sides in the disputes over the editorial policies of the CAD. But it was his conviction as to the value of the dictionary that made him ultimately always come out in defense of the enterprise and its editor-in-charge, as I will show in greater detail.

The second phase (1952–1957) of Gelb's ten-year plan was subdivided into the "first final phase" and the "second final phase." The first final phase included the redaction of articles, a task undertaken first by Landsberger and Oppenheim as a joint project, while the junior staff was still collecting words—mainly from lexical texts—and bibliographical references to them. As Landsberger put it: "The megalomaniac Dictionary project is pursued by Oppenheim with a great lack of enthusiasm, Gelb issues theoretical guidelines and hopes to find needy emigrants to work on it; I function as a meddling kibitzer."[56]

Given Landsberger's interest in families of words and semantic fields and Oppenheim's in material culture (the previously mentioned *Wörter und Sachen* approach), they chose to study the names of trees, taking these from the Sumerian-Akkadian bilingual vocabulary known as HAR-ra = hubullu, which has a topical arrangement. They began with the first entry in the third tablet comprising names of trees, the name for boxwood, *taskarinnu*. Soon, however, this topical orientation was given up in order to concentrate on the letter of the alphabet that the editors decided should be the first to be published, the letter H.

THE STANDARD OPERATING PROCEDURE

The choice of the editors for beginning the redaction of the CAD fell on the letter H (commonly transcribed in Assyriology as Ḫ) because words beginning with H occupied exactly one file cabinet out of the twenty that contained the lexical files. It was therefore assumed that words beginning with H represented one twentieth of the Akkadian vocabulary and thus Volume H would be an "average" volume.

The choice of this letter was based not only on its length, which was considered average, but also on the editors' conviction that it did not present the ambiguity that some other consonant, for which both a voiced and a voiceless variety existed, could have presented. (In those cases, if the voice of the consonant was unknown, upon Gelb's suggestion the voiced variety was preferred in the CAD.) Naturally, H too proved to be full of ambiguities: partly as this consonant represented one of the glottal or pharyngeal consonants of the Semitic roster, for example, aleph, ayin, ghayin and partly due to the large number of homophones that arose precisely as a result of such multiple etymologies.

More vexing was the question of establishing the organization and the format of the dictionary article. It was laid out in Gelb's Standard Operating Procedure (SOP), a document that did not find favor with the other members of the Dictionary team.

Gelb's SOP consisted of two parts: a theoretical part, and sample articles comprising *šaṭāru* (to write) and a few derivatives of the same root. The SOP contained a variety of practical guidelines, including such items as the spacing between lines, the number of carbon copies, and lists of abbreviations. Gelb also suggested that the author of a dictionary article sign and date the article, even though he admitted that this information might not appear in the printed version.

More important, the SOP laid out, in 110 points, directions for the presentation of—in Gelb's favored terminology—the lemma. A further 31 points were devoted, as Appendix I, to the system of transliteration and transcription and, as Appendixes II–IX, to

bibliographical and other abbreviations. He divided this presentation into 14 sections: I. Head. II. Grammatical category. III. Periods
and areas of attestation. IV. Cross references. V. Etymology. VI.
Morphology. VII. Orthography. VIII. Sumerian correspondences.
IX. Synonyms and antonyms. X. Semasiology. XI. Extraneous
sources. XII. Notes and discussions. XIII. Bibliography. XIV. Date
and signature.

An organization of such comprehensiveness and tightness was in
character for Gelb, whose linguistic formation was based on the
post-Bloomfieldian structural linguistics that dominated the early
1950s, a neatly laid out theory that appealed to Gelb's sense of order
and symmetry. It found no echo among the Dictionary team. When
the SOP was distributed in spring 1954 among the members of the
editorial board and the staff (Hallock, Reiner, Rowton) for comments, the staff made minor suggestions, while Oppenheim at first
refused to involve himself in the process. Only at Landsberger's
urging did he subsequently make his position known.

Differences in the presentation might have been ironed out, especially since neither Landsberger nor Oppenheim attached too much
importance to such technical details as paragraphing, the style of
abbreviations, and the use of "cf." versus "see." Unfortunately, the
word chosen by Gelb—and sent out to Assyriologists all over—was
much too complex to be a sample entry. The errors contained in it—
pointed out by Landsberger in a thirteen-page memorandum not
distributed beyond the CAD staff—would, it was feared, damage
the reputation of the Chicago project and may have been the reason
for Gelb's reluctance to announce the progress of the CAD project
in 1954 in Cambridge, England. Moreover, its complicated organization raised doubts in the mind of many colleagues around the
world about the feasibility of a dictionary along this model altogether. Oppenheim considered the distribution of the SOP and
especially the inclusion in it of the sample article a "tactical mistake" (in the letter to Jacobsen cited p. 30). Landsberger stated in
1954 (in a letter to Oppenheim) that "Gelb's SOP must be *rejected* as
too complicated, too rigid, and not practical."[57]

Landsberger, nevertheless, gave serious consideration to Gelb's
proposals and made a number of suggestions, not only on questions of detail—how to deal with foreign words, for example—but
on matters of principle too. He warned:

> A dictionary involving so many basic problems can not content itself with a
> simple arrangement of *loci probandi*; otherwise the writer of the article will not
> be able to resist the temptation to transform the grouping of the occurrences
> into a deduction of the meaning; he will proceed in a heuristic way from the

known to the unknown, instead of (as is demanded) from the simple to the complex.[58]

His "principles and postulates"[59] were enthusiastically endorsed by Gelb. It was also Landsberger who presented a "scheme for an article" compared and contrasted with the organization of Gelb's *ṣaṭaru*.

Landsberger then sets out his understanding of the aims of the Dictionary: It should be "a guide and *vade mecum* for the advanced Assyriologist in his struggling with the difficulties of his texts"; its secondary aims are to serve scholars of neighboring disciplines, such as historians of culture (to make accessible legal terms better to understand the Mesopotamian judicial system, and the like). "The user expects from it primarily not a nice ordering of well-known facts, but he seeks help in the uncounted cases where the meaning of a word is not known, ill-determined or where the proposals made differ each from the other." Landsberger also spelled out what he saw as the contrast between the CAD project and von Soden's lexicography (as manifested in various journal articles before the publication of his *Akkadisches Handwörterbuch*):

> in determining the meanings he possesses a good grasp and common sense; he is audacious, but at the same time sober; but what he lacks is the feeling for the niceties of style, context, situation, etc. (so-called Fingerspitzengefühl); accordingly his solutions are in many cases forced; von Soden has no interest whatsoever in the subtleties of legal conceptions or in the reconstruction of the material culture...

Further desiderata mentioned by Landsberger:

> Many classes of nouns, as gathered in the series HAR-ra, URU-anna, LÚ-ša, call for synoptic and systematic treatment; three attempts in this direction were made by staff members (Oppenheim, Landsberger, working on trees; Jacobsen on social classes); they were discontinued because they proceeded much too slowly to be of material help to the Dictionary. Another attempt, namely to digest the diagnostical omina in order to obtain a better grasp of the names of the parts of the body and the physiological verbs, undertaken by Oppenheim and me, ended with meagre results.

And he adds, "Our 'empirical' dictionary should be supplied with an etymological dictionary as an appendix." Landsberger also included a lengthy discussion on the concept of "root" in Akkadian.

Landsberger tried, as he often did, to bridge the gap between members of the editorial board. In his remarks, he urged Oppenheim to take part in the discussion of the SOP:

> Mr. O. did not contribute a single remark on SOP, thus expressing his view that only the spirit of the workers counts and that they can easily submit themselves to any external shape of the articles. I cannot share his point of view: the principles established in SOP are by no means irrelevant nor should they be considered as unchangeable.… I hope that Oppenheim, the only one who has produced a considerable number of articles for the project, will overcome his aversion to theoretical talks and take his stand.

Upon this, Oppenheim felt obliged to participate in the discussion after all. He gave his opinion, not on the SOP but on Landsberger's comments on the SOP, as follows:

> The real difference [between Landsberger and Gelb] lies deeper: the relationship of the discussion (argumentation) of meanings on one side and the presentation of the quotations on the other side. Landsberger demands with vigor that the argumentation should precede the enumeration of references. Gelb, however, wants first to present the evidence with all references and then the discussion. It is rather obvious that both these "systems" reflect the individual psychological make-up of their originators; Landsberger prefers the dogmatic approach that is an adequate expression of his scholarly standing and temper, while Gelb wishes to follow the "objectivity" of the American linguistic school.
>
> Personally, I do think that *both* approaches create an artificial separation of a whole which is the argumentation of the meaning on the basis of the passages incorporated in the presentation exactly as it is traditional in lexical research, not only in Assyriology, but also in classical studies.

Still, he admitted that this "holistic" approach may lead to articles becoming too long and reflecting "too much the individual style of the writer and thus mar the uniformity essential for a dictionary."[60]

Gelb's plan for the organization of the articles was vitiated by the errors in the sample articles; instead of presenting the future Dictionary in a favorable light, the premature dissemination of the SOP manuscript among Assyriologists all over the world proved an embarrassment. Consequently, even the theoretical part of the SOP, which could have been debated, did not receive the attention it deserved. It may have been a case of throwing out the baby with the bathwater, even though several of Gelb's points were retained in the eventual publication. Gelb, however, was not ready to accept major changes to his outline, so much so that when the manuscript of Volume H came up for vote to the editors in August 1955, Gelb alone, while voting "yes" on the volume's substance, voted "no" on its form. In practice, words in CAD volumes do have a "heading" that includes, although not necessarily in this order, Gelb's sections I, II, III, IV, VI, VII, but not sections V (Etymology, which Gelb himself did not consider essential) and IX; section VIII is given more prominence. It is Section X, Semasiology, that proved to be the longest and most detailed part of the lemma (the dictionary entry) in the published volumes. In the sample articles included in Gelb's SOP, translations of cited texts were few. In the sample *šaṭāru*, for example, the first nine sections occupy four pages, and the tenth, Semasiology, nine. By contrast, in Volume Š published in 1992 the "heading" and the "Sumerian correspondences" of *šaṭāru* take up one column of the page, and the meaning section, fifteen pages (thirty columns).

Oppenheim laid out his conception of the treatment of a word's meaning, in particular relating to verbs that have diverse stem forms: "My experience with the verb *hasāsu* has taught me that only the arrangement according to meaning [and not according to stem form] leads to a satisfactory presentation without repetitions. … I propose to list at the head of the article all established meanings as diversified as they may be, in the very sequence as they are treated. The reader may deduce for himself what is called 'basic meaning'. This simplifies our task and serves as a kind of index to the meanings discussed."[61] Such a structure of the dictionary article, moreover, made it easier for the nonspecialist to find the meaning or nuance sought.

It is quite clear that for Landsberger and Oppenheim the elucidation of the word's *meaning* was of primary importance, whereas for Gelb the orderly presentation of the evidence was crucial.

In lieu of theoretical discussions, Richard Hallock, at the time the CAD's editorial secretary, presented a memo in February 1955 on the "Current Style in Writing of Articles." It can be summarized as follows: The articles start with a heading giving the grammatical information and the chronological and geographical distribution (paragraph 1); this is followed by a section citing equivalences from Sumerian and Akkadian vocabularies and bilingual texts, and other scholia, if any (paragraph 2).

The most important section is Hallock's treatment of "Text Citations" (paragraph 3):

> Normally each citation is to be accompanied by a translation. Where a translated citation is followed by others which can be readily understood from the first, the latter need not be translated—in such cases use the form: (translated citation), and cf. (second citation), also (third citation). Where there is more than one meaning, the citations will be grouped according to the meanings given in paragraph 1. At the beginning of each group the meaning will be repeated in *exactly* the form used in paragraph 1. Every citation must belong clearly to one of these meanings.
>
> Where a further subdivision according to nuances or usages is clearly called for, the subdivisions will be lettered a, b, c, etc., and titled (the subdivision titles will not be indicated in paragraph 1). When a meaning is subdivided, every citation under that meaning must belong clearly to one of the subdivisions; where necessary, subdivisions titled "gen. mng." or "other occ." can be used.

In paragraph 3 [Text Citations] there should be no general discussion (that belongs in paragraph 4), and as little special discussion as possible.[62]

I cannot establish whether Hallock's outline is a modification of Gelb's original SOP, or whether it was compiled *post factum*, on the basis of the actual practice in Volume 6 (H), from which his examples were taken. On the whole, the style described by Hallock is still "current" and rightly so, in that it provides some fixed coordinates for the "drafter" of the dictionary article. Of course, the crucial point remains the establishment and the organization of the word's meaning or meanings, and for this reason most articles of the CAD—except those dealing with words of the material culture of no clearly established meaning which are glossed only "a stone," "a piece of apparel," "a plant," and the like—are highly individualistic.

THE LETTER H

The first words written for the H volume were structured according to Gelb's guidelines as articulated in his SOP. A few of these drafts were preserved, "for historical purposes," by Oppenheim. These drafts—all treating short words—bear the names of the "drafter," of Oppenheim who edited them, and of Gelb who did further editing and sometimes added etymological or comparative material. A final copyediting was done by Hallock. [63]

Drafts written by the junior staff (me and Rowton) were edited by Oppenheim, in a process that is more accurately described by "rewrite" but that still goes under the name "editing" today. It consists of revising the organization of the dictionary article, improving or even radically changing the translations of the cited passages, adding material that escaped the "drafter" or that had been discovered more recently, as well as the more technical aspect of seeing to it that the article conforms to certain editorial conventions. The latter function was eventually to become the responsibility of the editorial secretary, later also called assistant to the editor(s) and manuscript editor.

After a first year of drudgery, consisting mainly of writing bibliographical cards but eventually also parsing and filing bilingual vocabularies, I graduated to writing drafts. Drafts more often than not had to be based on cards that were antiquated, prepared in the 1930s and 1940s from inadequately published and understood texts; this has been the case throughout the life of the Dictionary. Cards often contained only the keyword and the reference so that the context had to be established before a stab could be made at the meaning. A similar situation prevails even today. No wonder the drafts are often unsatisfactory, and the editor needs to rewrite the word.

The editor-in-charge may be expected to "streamline" the articles written by the various collaborators. Nevertheless, the editor often leaves the organization of the word as the drafter conceived it, and makes only minor corrections in the transcription and translation; this may be done out of respect for a colleague's judgment or with the intention of providing a variety of views to the readers. Indeed, it sometimes happens that the identity of the drafter can be established from the printed dictionary article.

So can, of course, the identity of the editor, since articles also reflect the interests, the competence, in short the personality of the editor-in-charge. Some editors are more conservative, not to say timorous, and prefer more literal, down-to-earth translations. Others are more easily given to flights of fancy; they favor—or permit to stand—translations that are more free, even too free in the eyes of some colleagues, but that in their opinion better render the intent of the author and the flavor of the original. Oppenheim belonged to the latter group, and he was quite explicit about his endeavor, in the "Essay on Translating Akkadian Texts"[64] for which he chose the motto "Can these bones live?"

In the beginning, it was the different categories of meaning that determined the organization of the article, not the word's grammatical category or function, as stated by Oppenheim in his comments on the SOP (see previous chapter). This organizational principle, operative in Volume H, was subsequently abandoned, possibly because the word's meaning often changed according to its grammatical category. On the other hand, another principle that was never explicitly stated, the juxtaposition of similar quotations without regard to their chronological distribution, survived much longer. Citations from various periods were mixed intentionally to show recurrent themes and phraseology; for example, that Nabonidus (middle of the first millennium BCE) echoed Hammurapi (who reigned a thousand years earlier). Even this practice survived only in especially striking cases, as later drafters and editors tended to favor the chronological sequence, no doubt influenced by the practice of the *Akkadisches Handwörterbuch*.

Before I joined the Assyrian Dictionary Project, my professors in Paris gave me the excellent advice to read as many texts as possible. In this way I developed not only an acquaintance with the various genres of Akkadian texts, but also a sense for what is and what is not grammatically and contextually possible, though—of course—never to the degree that Landsberger had. I was also, young as I was, firmly convinced of the correctness of my views, an attitude fostered by Oppenheim who was always ready with praise but looked askance at by some members of the Editorial Board and the Dictionary staff. I repaid Oppenheim's trust by working very hard to help him complete the manuscript of the first volume of the CAD, without fully realizing at that time the crucial importance of this step.

That my work during the hectic months of finishing the H volume was valuable in quality as well as in quantity I found out only after my retirement, as I sifted through the correspondence of Landsberger in preparation for this account. There I found the following comment: "… I got involved in this mad rush for which Reiner has developed a matchless acrobatic talent (lightning swift, but not sloppy or by halves). I continue to function as errordetector and as lexicographer in the traditional sense."[65]

The edited words, according to the previous agreement of the editors, were circulated to the other members of the editorial board. Some proposed just a few changes, but Landsberger liked to delve into the core of the subject and, often after lengthy discussions with Jacobsen, sometimes wrote what amounted to a small monograph on the topic. This process, of course, threatened to upset the timeframe agreed upon by the editorial board and thus Oppenheim's plans for prompt publication. As Landsberger wrote to Kraus: "I now have spent four months rewriting all the articles on the roots h$^{\flat}_x$y. I had to do it because they were so bad."[66] The volume, nevertheless, progressed well, indeed so well that Oppenheim could make the announcement in August 1954 in Cambridge, England, that H was ready in first draft and its publication was foreseen within one year or two.

It was to be expected that the announcement would be made by Gelb; indeed in a letter of June 28, 1954, to Director Kraeling, Margaret Bell reported that "The Linguistic Institute[67] is going great guns, with all the great men on the third floor taking turns sitting at each other's feet. Erica [Reiner] gives me reports on this, midst her frantic efforts to attend the seminars and also write the Dictionary, the letter H of which she is attempting to finish in time for Jay [Gelb] to announce it to the Congress in August."

The announcement was made at a special "dictionary" meeting of Assyriologists to discuss the "Marburg agreement" that circumscribed the roles of the two dictionaries, the German one under the editorship of Wolfram von Soden and the CAD. It fell to Oppenheim to make this announcement because Gelb's report was noncommittal and did not mention the CAD's achievements, whereas the assembled Assyriologists expected information about the actual progress of the project.

It would be impossible to reconstruct the events of the Cambridge meeting, since all the participants are dead, were it not for the fortunate preservation of an exchange of letters between Oppenheim and Jacobsen. Oppenheim reported on the Dictionary meeting to Jacobsen, who had stayed in Chicago, and Jacobsen, in his reply, gave him reassurance. Neither letter is dated, although it is not difficult to place them in August 1954.

Dear Thorkild,

Just returned from the Congress and while my memory is still fresh, I would like to report to you on the two meetings concerned with the Dictionary Project. For Wednesday (the 25th) afternoon, a lecture of Gelb had been announced with considerable emphasis by Gadd and it was to be followed by a closed meeting of the International Advisory Committee. In many conversations and private discussions, the expectation was expressed by all Assyriologists (including Gadd, the president of the section) that the state and the aims of the Project would be presented by Gelb and I consequently was very careful not to discuss Dictionary problems with anybody before that date. The paper was announced as "Main Problems of Akkadian Lexicography."[68] To the obvious dismay of his audience Gelb presented nothing but his usual "line" of linguistic platitudes about lexicography—lexicology, a protracted report on the history of dictionary-making, and a mass of unconnected remarks on his favorite topics; only accidentally he mentioned that it was too early to speak of any publication. The talk was followed by a long and embarrassing silence which the presiding Mr. Nougayrol had a hard time to break. Finally, Landsberger suggested that Mr. Gelb should tell the audience about the Chicago Project, its situation, plans, etc. To this Gelb reacted with some noncommittal phrases which seemed to me only to aggravate the embarrassment of the situation. For this reason, I found it necessary to say a few words to the subject matter which the audience—rightly or wrongly—seemed to expect.

I said that there was no reason to be unduly pessimistic about the project, that it was run by a board of editors (which nobody knew) and that these editors have recently voted upon and adopted a plan which aims at publishing the letter H (ready by now in the first draft) within one year or two and to continue the publication in this method and speed. Mr. Nougayrol then closed the discussion with some generalities.

What I wanted to convey to the audience was the very answer to the unspoken question in everybody's mind as to the future of the Dictionary and to the chances to make it available to the Assyriologists. I also wanted to dispel the impression that the Project was completely and solely in the hands of a scholar much more interested in academic questions of the theory of dictionary-making, the mannerisms of its mechanics, etc., than in producing a useful tool within a reasonable time. That very impression had been caused by the unfortunate and bulky SOP. Quite a number of colleagues told me that the size of the article on *šaṭāru* precluded any hope of ever seeing the dictionary; others commented rather satirically on its unnecessary and pedantic complicatedness. I do think that it was extremely ill timed to send the SOP and it was, by the way, against my wish that the *šaṭāru*-article was added to it. There is no point in sending out a sample with the unspoken understanding that the actual "merchandise" will be delivered in an entirely different style. It was a tactical mistake.

The so-called International Advisory Committee (Falkenstein, Goetze, von Soden, Pohl, Dossin, Gadd, Nougayrol, Landsberger, Gelb, and myself) met in what might be termed a mood of crisis. Gelb made an appeal for funds which caused one of these silly and rambling discussions about how to get money from the UNESCO, the Swedish Government, the Heidelberger Akademie der Wissenschaften, etc. Gelb also asked for advice concerning the arrangement of the words, etc. Suddenly Falkenstein asked for the release of von Soden since there seemed no reasonable hope that the Chicago Dictionary could be anywhere near ready by 1957. He was supported by Dossin and Pohl and the former even pressed for a vote on that issue. Here, Goetze was tactful enough to come to the aid of Gelb and opposed any vote since—as he said—it was obviously the sense of the meeting that the agreement was immoral as such and that the interest of Assyriology demands the publication of v.S.'s "short" Wörterbuch. Von Soden declared that he could be ready in 1957 or 1958 [in reality, publication of the *Akkadisches Handwörterbuch* was begun in 1959 and finished in 1981] and that money is available to publish his work immediately. Gelb then declared that there will be a reorganization of the entire Project on our return to Chicago and that the decision lies with Kraeling [the director of the Oriental Institute]. The meeting was adjourned.

I understand that Falkenstein is going to write directly to Kraeling to ask for the release of von Soden. The latter is going to Vienna so that his subsistence does not fall any more upon the German academies."

A handwritten answer to Oppenheim's letter from Jacobsen is not dated.

Dear Leo:

It was good to hear from you and very interesting to get such a full account of the Dictionary meetings. You did certainly a good job in saving what could be saved but essentially a slightly unfriendly attitude was probably to be expected. The average Assyriologist wants a dictionary quickly and gives little thought—at this time—to quality. To this comes, of course, the v. Soden issue, which strikes me as full of emotions—partly anti-American—that distort the factual situation. *Obviously* he must be released now that we cannot deliver as agreed. But the psychological reaction has been a bad one all along and we surely made a mistake in touching the matter at all. To all of this, then, comes Jay's individualistic kind of interests which are quite beyond the average Assyriologist. They seem impractical nonsense to him. You know yourself how long it takes one to see what Jay is really driving at and to see the basic importance of it behind the theoretical and "linguistic" nonsense. As for the SOP and the *šaṭāru* article Benno may have told you that I protested against sending it off with no authorization and without any check. Jay just went ahead and sent it off. However, that is water over the dam. He—no less than von Soden— should be allowed to publish his stuff. But I am glad you told about the Board and its responsibilities. I am really very optimistic Leo. Looking at the facts of the situation they have never been better. The h-volume is ready in its first draft. Benno and I must finish our part in about half a year from October. At any rate, I am going to turn it in after 6 months whether I think I could do more to it or not. It should be really quite good when it goes to press and must have ever so much more than v. Soden can give on all kinds of points.

The spirit of the Dictionary is a crucial point. It can, I think, be managed. One necessary thing is for the board to become more active. The greatest achievement so far is the decision to publish by letter and to get the h-volume out. That we should follow up by taking the necessary steps to impose time limits and to make arrangements for editorial (Mrs. Hauser) treatment, etc. We should not leave the initiative to Jay. The type of publication should also be followed up. Further matters about the h-volume: The revision of the articles on the basis of Benno's and my suggestions could best, I think, be done by you. In this matter, and in the unavoidable difference of opinion that will arise you can count on more than normal cooperation and peacefulness from me.

These were exactly the words of reassurance and promise of cooperation and support that Oppenheim needed for going ahead with the plans for the H volume even in the absence of Landsberger— who was convalescing in England from a heart attack—and in the face of Gelb's reluctant cooperation. It is the more incomprehensible that Jacobsen's attitude changed so radically vis-a-vis Oppenheim and consequently the CAD between summer 1954 and fall 1958, a subject to which we will return. At the moment, however, Oppenheim was buoyed up by the prospect of bringing out the first volume of the Dictionary when, it seems, even the director of the Institute was skeptical about its future. When Oppenheim wrote to Landsberger in England on October 10, 1954 about the happenings since his return to Chicago, he reported on a proposal by Director Kraeling to assist von Soden's dictionary instead of going ahead with the Chicago project.[69] He added: "Jay remained curiously silent with regard to Carl's proposal—I have the definite impression that if it were not for his purely personal vanity, he would drop the dictionary rather today than tomorrow. However, he still thinks that his organization of the material as stated in the SOP is nothing short of perfect and refuses to compromise in any way."

Oppenheim himself was not too sure about the Dictionary's prospects, for which he foresaw having to fight both the director and Gelb, with help only from Landsberger and Jacobsen:

> I had many talks with Thorkild who, by the way, does very nice work on the articles and I only pray that his enthusiasm will last. He plans—so he told me— to ask, in the first meeting after your arrival, to force a vote on the proposal to charge me with the editing and "druckfertig-machung" [making ready for press] of the H volume within a given period of time during which he and you would work through the first draft. I agreed to this under the condition that my H manuscript has to be accepted by the entire board within two weeks of submission by vote and without qualifications or to be rejected in toto. This would give me the possibility to have the MS written (by Mr. Madsen [graduate student working as a typist] who is to return to us November 1st) not in the SOP pattern but in some way along your lines (I have concrete proposals) without any interference from Jay. This new "plan" would keep Gelb nominally in charge, the editorial board functioning and all details of editing outside the interference of the SOP. But will Jay concede to this loss of power? He is too intelligent to fail to see the real import of such a vote. If he goes to Karl in this matter we will only create there the impression of continuous quarreling and I think that Karl is rather tired of us and our troubles (see above). In short, I am not optimistic at all about the future of the project.[70]

In spite of his doubts, Kraeling wrote to Falkenstein on October 11, 1954, to release the German academies from the Marburg agreement, and Falkenstein responded in equally courteous terms. Kraeling's decision may have been influenced by Landsberger's letter from England, in which he urged such a move, stating:

> The explicit Dictionary [i.e., the CAD] is as necessary for Assyriology as the Kurzwörterbuch [i.e., von Soden's *Akkadisches Handwörterbuch*] is; it is a good project still and a good thing for the Institute, if all the SOPs and other fancies are abandoned and all this advertising (with nothing behind) by which the public has lost all confidence, is replaced by work and work again.[71]

Of the many problems that remained, in addition to those arising from the differences of personality, not the least was that much work remained to be done on H. Landsberger gave his support even from afar, from England, in two handwritten letters to Oppenheim; the second is dated November 10, 1954; the first letter is undatable because the first of its eleven closely written pages is missing, but it is probably from the end of October or the beginning of November 1954. It concerns the future of the CAD:

> I continue to consider the "constitution" of 1952, which came about as a result of my revolt, and which Jay has not yet been able to swallow and which he sabotages, apparently without effect after all, to be as correct and beneficial now as before.... You have the pivotal position and I cannot but support and help you. Firstly, the right to decide about the Dictionary must be reserved for those who have so far worked the most for it. Without minimizing my contribution, there is no doubt that it is you who had by far the largest share in it. The share of the other members of the editorial board has to be evaluated realistically. Your innate modesty must tell you to what extent you have the right to take part in the discussion. An "Oversight Board" can only be helpful, and Karl [Kraeling] must be free to solicit objective judgments such as those of Güterbock, Goetze, Speiser.
>
> "All right" is what someone would say who has followed me willingly so far. "But is quantity everything? Does the danger not exist that our Leo will let himself be pressed into a hectic rush, to finish at any price? Especially if he sees before him a higher goal, such as a cultural history?" I answer as follows:
> 1. None of us can avoid making some ad hoc decisions and cutting Gordian knots; this quality is especially characteristic of our rival von Soden.
> 2. Leo knows that we are engaged in a scientific project and that this involves the need to work *in peace* on the problems.
> 3. So long as Landsberger is active, he gives a certain guaranty; moreover, it is Leo's custom to talk over the problems with his colleagues.
> 4. If this point is crucial, then the project must be abandoned.
> *Tactics*:
> a) Leo must decide, after serious consideration, whether he wishes to assume the Dictionary as his life's task. It is to be expected that there will be left for him a considerable lifetime for other tasks.
> b) Karl must be persuaded; it is not enough to extort from him a lame "yes" or tacit consent. He and his eventual consultants (whom I can easily influence and whose opinion—which agrees with mine—I have already

partly sought) can only be convinced if a *Dictionary* is produced and not letters spewed forth; if it can be made plausible to him (them) that it is not a duplication of von Soden's opus.

c) In the Board the majority of 3:1 must be used ruthlessly. First, Gelb's SOP must be discarded as too complicated, too rigid, and not practical; then the Landsberger-Oppenheim SOP, which I request to be formulated by my return (short, but not too vague), accepted; then the general procedure for the future work decided, similarly using majority vote.

Please do not use crooked paths, no surprise attack on Jay, no "tactics"; no situation where one ox pulls the team in one direction, the other in another! This lack of clarity, cowardice, double talk was the sole cause of the poisoning of the third floor's atmosphere. To be sure, Jay was always a comfortable excuse for our own inefficiency, lack of interest, for that matter the avoidance of confessing that the entire project is unripe and megalomaniac.

On the other hand, we three and every other Assyriologist agree that Jay is not the person to head a team that makes an Akkadian dictionary. Now already, after a relatively short period of time, he has shown that all he can do is organize it to death. He can boss neither experts of our caliber nor the young collaborators, who should not be bossed but directed by experienced experts. If Thorkild and you believe that leaving Jay out in the cold is unseemly out of friendship and other personal grounds, then I would recommend that the project be utterly abandoned and that possible substitute projects so formulated that Jay's domain is clearly delimited from ours. But perhaps this point of view is not conclusive because Karl is the ideal doctor for such "cold cures" and perhaps even Jay begins to realize that his true strength and future lies not in the field of semasiology."[72]

Still, Landsberger argued against publishing each letter as an individual fascicle of the CAD. He advocated postponing publication until the letters a–h were ready for the printer, but to avoid misunderstanding having *all* (emphasis Landsberger's) articles "absolutely ready for press" [in absolut druckfertigem Zustand] before the printing of this first fascicle a–h.

Landsberger did not neglect the youngest collaborator either: In a charming letter in answer to my good wishes for his recovery, he struck a wistful note:

> But you will not doubt my sincerity when I state that invariably the nicest spot of the world for me is Orinst No 309,[73] better with than without dirt and tobacco-smell and even better with than without the Dictionary and the whole of its 'Problematik'…. I am quite confident that our good cooperation will continue, perhaps under better conditions. Your Šurpu should be the model of an edition and I shall be happy indeed, if you honour me to promote you to Ph.D., the last but not least of a long row.[74]

The same sentiments were repeated in Landsberger's answer to Oppenheim's letter of October 10:

> As I already wrote to Erika, Orinst 309 is for me the nicest place of residence and the third floor—in spite of everything—the favorite milieu. I am pleased to see from your letter that these sympathies are not completely one-sided.[75]

Landsberger's "constitution" of 1952 was changed in December 1954, when Kraeling, upon the request of the Board of Editors, appointed four editors (Gelb, Jacobsen, Landsberger, and Oppenheim), each for a term of one year, and one editor-in-charge for a term of three years. Upon the Board's recommendation, Oppenheim was appointed editor-in-charge.[76] In its report to the director of the Institute, the Board summarized the "major steps in preparation of a volume" as: (1) Preparation of first draft by the Dictionary assistants under direction of the editor-in-charge and in consultation with the editors whenever needed. (2) Recasting of the articles by the editors. (3) Preparation of final draft by the editor-in-charge. (4) Final approval of MS by board. [77]

The background of this reorganization was described in Kraeling's letter to Alexander Heidel, the Assyriologist and Biblical scholar, who was in Iraq:

> Since you left all kinds of interesting things have been happening up on the third floor of the Institute. The Assyrian Dictionary had another blow-up and reorganization. The impass between Benno and Jay became deeper as the result of the Cambridge meeting and it was obvious that we would make no progress in the direction of actual publication unless we had a new deal. The new deal is now established and Leo has taken over the reins as editor in charge. Also there is to be new clerical assistance for the undertaking. Also Leo has been recommended for appointment to full professorial rank, a well-deserved promotion. Part of the inevitable shake-up was the return of Dick Hallock to full time on the Dictionary work...[78]

With the cooperation of Landsberger and Jacobsen assured, and with the tacit agreement of Gelb, Oppenheim forged ahead with the H volume. While the Assyriologists worked on the entries, arrangements needed to be made for publication. The logical choice was the University of Chicago Press. The Press, however, expressed little interest and put little faith in the prospects of the enterprise and would not commit to printing more than 500 copies. Instead, the publishing firm J. J. Augustin, Glückstadt, Germany, was approached, at Oppenheim's initiative. The firm had been founded in 1632 and was well known as the publisher of such distinguished series as the Dumbarton Oaks and the Institute of Fine Arts volumes. Director Kraeling conducted the discussions with J. J. Augustin, on which he reported in a letter sent from New Haven, Connecticut, June 28, 1955. (See Appendix 3.) A four-page sample was needed by August 14, and the manuscript by November 1; the publication date announced by Augustin's flyer was April 1956. Between the head of the firm, "J. J.", and Oppenheim there sprang up a working friendship that endured and continued under their successors, Jack Augustin and myself, until well into the 1990s.

Before the first volume went to press, a sample quire of H was typeset by J. J. Augustin and distributed to Assyriologists around the world. It contained the announcement of the publication, the title page, and one page with the words *halu*, *hâlu* A, and *hâlu* B. (see page 41) That was when the thunder struck. While suggestions and criticism were expected, the number of mistakes found in the single page of quotes was staggering. Fritz Rudolf Kraus, the often referred-to former student of Landsberger's, professor of Assyriology in Leiden, not only took exception to some of the CAD's decisions about format[79] but he also took the trouble to check every single quote in the sample page and found countless errors in the references and occasionally in the quotes themselves. The Chicago team was shocked. Our confidence was shattered: we never imagined the manuscript would contain so many mistakes. It became clear that the manuscript of H, ready as it was, could not be published without revisions. This experience had the salutary effect that the editors decided that henceforth every reference was to be checked against the cuneiform original *after* the manuscript was typed and *before* it went to press, a practice that continues to this day.

While the editors had not imagined that H—at least the sample—could be so bad, there was nothing to be done but to go ahead with it. And go ahead they did. The references obviously had to be checked for accuracy, but questions of format, brought up both internally and through the comments of the readers of the sample page, had to take back seat to the now ever more important publication of the first fruits of the CAD. To that aim, the staff often worked evenings and weekends, even enlisting the help of Mrs. Oppenheim for such tasks as proofreading and creating cross references. It was, according to the working style of Oppenheim, a race against the clock. Here the good personal relations with Augustin were a great asset. "Augustin assures Leo" said Margaret Bell in her letter of March 29, 1956, to Kraeling, "that a copy of the Dictionary will be bound and ready for the A.O.S. meeting in Baltimore. That means that the last 3 signatures of revised page proof will leave here March 31, arrive Germany Tues. April 3, leave Germany bound Sat. 6th, and be in Baltimore the 9th. What a man and what a schedule. I paid the second installment of $1500 today. He sure has earned it. As of today there are orders for 87 copies."

First, of course, the manuscript of H had to be finished and approved by the Editorial Board. The formal approval was to take place, by written vote, on August 1, 1955, according to a motion passed on Wednesday, June 22, 1955, at 2:00 p.m. in the presence of the director of the Oriental Institute. Nevertheless, on August 3, Kraeling, in letters addressed to each member of the Editorial Board, had to remind the Board of its promise. Thereupon, the editors turned in their votes: all four editors voted "yes" on content, but on the question of form only three; Gelb, alone, voted "no."

Even the final style of the printed volume needed to be established. Kraeling's secretary Fritzi forwarded to him one copy of "each style of Assyrian Dictionary proofs," on September 1, 1955. She also reports the appointment of the new editorial secretary: "We have got Miss Bowman for the Dictionary, " and "Things are boiling and steaming upstairs. No one can quite accept the fact that publication approaches." Not to be outdone in the news department, Margaret Bell wrote to Kraeling on September 6, 1955, among other items, "Miss Reiner is now a Ph.D.... The first draft of the letter E was finished by Rowton right on schedule.... The Assyrian Dictionary is relatively calm."

To improve the quality of the dictionary, Oppenheim, possibly worried by the mistakes detected in the sample page of H, decided to submit the articles, in final manuscript or in galleys, to nonresident Assyriologists for comments. The first reader was W. G. Lambert, then at the University of Toronto, whose suggestions for improvement are acknowledged in the Foreword to Volume G. Besides Lambert—who read the manuscript—other colleagues read the words in galley proofs; the role of all these contributors is laid out in greater detail in the section on Outside Readers.

Advice and encouragement also came from Oppenheim's old friend and colleague, Abraham Sachs, professor at Brown University. Sachs was that ideal reader who, by his own admission, read each volume of the CAD cover to cover, as soon as it was published; he read not to criticize but to learn and, whenever possible, contribute from his knowledge. While his special competence lay in Babylonian mathematical and astronomical texts, his interests and curiosity were wide ranging, and his memory, as well as his files, prodigious. His previous connection with the CAD (1939–1941) led him to appreciate the work that had gone into these volumes; he was, at that juncture of the CAD's progress, the ideal concerned but sympathetic reader. Often, instead of pointing out errors or additional data, he anticipated subsequent volumes and sent to Oppenheim references from both published and unpublished texts. Some of his contributions are acknowledged in the pertinent articles of the Dictionary, for example, under *akāmu*

A 'mist', *naṣāru* 'to keep watch for celestial phenomena', *naštuk* (a leather bag); for other corrections and contributions he did not receive—or ask for—any credit.

It was only after the publication of Volume H that questions of format came up again. They involved such decisions as selection of typefaces (bold face for keywords, smaller font size for references) and of paragraphing with and without indentations, all arising from the layout of the H volume that was deemed confusing and unsatisfactory. Abbreviations and cross-referencing also needed revision. The changes were adopted in the subsequent volumes, so that H has a completely different look from Volume G, which followed it immediately (1956), and from all the other volumes, preceding or following H in the alphabet. An early decision was to use the well-established acronyms for journals but to quote books with the name of the author and a short, typical word or two of the title. This practice elicited the approval of Albrecht Goetze of Yale University who had founded "a society against unintelligible abbreviations," but it infuriated some European scholars who could not see why they should pay for the extra paper necessary for printing lengthy references. Oppenheim simply said that anybody who has produced a book deserves to have his or her name stated. The CAD still adheres to that principle.

The problems of format, style, accuracy, coverage, and other issues stemming from the nature of the then current state of Assyriology and from the particular approach sought and eventually adopted by the Dictionary were not the only, nor the most grievous, problems that confronted the CAD. The project was to weather several crises between 1955 and 1959, and again in 1960–1962. While in the course of various reorganizations the duties and responsibilities of the editorial board—consisting of Gelb, Jacobsen, Landsberger, and Oppenheim—were laid down, voted upon, and approved and sanctioned by the director of the Oriental Institute, resentments were building up against the manner in which Leo Oppenheim, the editor-in-charge, ran the project. These resentments persisted even though on repeated occasions the members of the board, often at the initiative of Thorkild Jacobsen, voted to give Oppenheim the responsibility for editing the volume being worked on and even several more volumes.[80]

Each of the members of the board had his own reasons for objecting to Oppenheim's way of proceeding. Gelb had not yet overcome his disappointment on having had to concede that the Dictionary could and would move forward on a new track (as he stated in the Foreword to A/1, p. xix: "Gelb went on a leave of absence for one year, which was prolonged indefinitely due to his inability or unwillingness to adjust to the new spirit prevailing in the Dictionary"), though he soon found new outlets for his creativity in other projects. He eventually also enjoyed serving as the expert on linguistic matters and on early texts (on Old Akkadian, but also on Old Babylonian royal inscriptions for which he had not only an extensive bibliography but also transliterations that he strove to keep up to date) when he was consulted, not least at Oppenheim's prompting, by the Dictionary staff. Landsberger principally objected to the speed of the enterprise, for which he coined the phrase "insane haste," half in jest but rooted in his attitude toward scholarship that required what he called "affectionate immersion."[81] The phrase "insane haste", and various complaints about the "hectic pace" of the CAD, often came up in his correspondence with Kraus. In an early letter he reports to Kraus that Oppenheim has officially taken over as editor-in-charge for three years, although as editor for one year only, just like the other three members of the board.

> My task is to review and make ready for press the drafts delivered by Oppi, Reiner, Rowton. It is furthered but also aggravated by the fact that Jacobsen is part and parcel of it, and that I discuss with him the Sumerian he adduces just as I do everything else. The big question is whether we are fast enough to keep up the speed promised by Oppi.[82]

Oppenheim was trying to adhere to a timetable and thus often reclaimed the Dictionary manuscript from the other editors before they finished their review of it. He also neglected to keep up the weekly "staff meetings" in which various issues were supposed to be discussed and which could have served to vent the staff's feelings; instead, he went to see each staff member individually to discuss policy or practical matters.

In the end, it was Thorkild Jacobsen who, after having initially given his support to the project and to its director, found that he could not go along with it; tragically, he chose not simply to withdraw but to try to stop the project altogether. At first, he could be swayed from his negative attitude. In June 1956, Margaret Bell wrote to Director Kraeling: "The work on gimel [G] proceeds on schedule, with the MS due to be sent off to Augustin on July 15. I get to be so proud of Leo and Erica and the others. Thorkild has ceased to try to resist and is keeping up with the work handed to him."

Jacobsen's objections centered on the lack of time allowed to Landsberger—with whom he discussed the Dictionary and various other scholarly matters every afternoon[83]—to revise the CAD manuscript; on the high-handedness of the editor-in-charge; and on the many errors remaining in consequence in the final manuscript and even in the published volumes. All these stemmed, according to Jacobsen, from the dictatorial way in which the editor-in-charge ran the Dictionary project, instead of following the American constitutional system of checks and balances.

Deeper differences lay under the surface. Jacobsen had certain ideas about Mesopotamian religion that were first expressed by him in the volume edited by Henri Frankfort, *Before philosophy, the intellectual adventure of ancient man: An essay on speculative thought in the ancient Near East,* and eventually expanded in his *Treasures of Darkness,* published, finally, in 1976. Before his ideas appeared in print under his own name, he tried to include them under appropriate vocabulary entries, so to speak endorsed by the CAD. Since Jacobsen's major attack was directed at the E volume, perhaps it came down after all to "whether the king slept with the *entu*-priestess or not," as our Viennese friend Hans Zeisel, professor at the University of Chicago's Law School, put it.

Another deep-seated difference between Oppenheim and his co-editors was Oppenheim's "aversion to theoretical talks," to use Landsberger's words, and his conviction—again in Landsberger's words—"that only the spirit of the workers counts and that they can easily submit themselves to any external shape of the articles";[84] while Gelb believed that order and organization were already halfway to achieving results. In the end it was Oppenheim, generally regarded as the dreamer, who showed practical sense when, as stated in the Foreword to H, "faced with the grave choice of whether to strive for maximal penetration in depth with publication in the indefinite future, or to make an orderly though not always definitive presentation of the accumulated material within the reasonably near future , [he] decided for the latter" Volume 6 (H), p. vii. It was the example of the MED that gave the necessary underpinning to his decision, but it was his passion, exemplified in his motto *navigare necesse est, vivere non est necesse*[85] (to sail is necessary; to live is not necessary), that impelled him to stay, undaunted, with the project for twenty years, until his death.

(handwritten: ← Sample Page) 10 pt ½ lett. ... 6-8 larger)

(handwritten right margin: set in 9-pt. bold face Roman)

ḫālu

ḫālu s.; maternal uncle; OAkk., OB, OA.

ḫa-a-lu = a-ḫu-um-mu brother-of-the-mother Malku I 125.

(a) in gen.: PN ḫa-al-šu PN his maternal uncle MDP 24 376:9. (b) in PN: Ḫa-lum MDP 2 pl. 3 xv 16, OAkk.; DINGIR-ḫa-lum PSBA 33 pl. 43 No. 17:6, OB; A-bu-um-ḫa-lum YOS 8 98:47, OB, also Corpus of Ancient Near Eastern Seals 1 No. 326, SLB 1/2 4:23; Ša-lim-ḫa-li-im (genitive) TCL 20 176:12, OA; Ḫa-li-ma-ra-aš UET 4 521:1, OB, note: I-gi-ḫa-lum CT 32 10 i 23, Ur III and passim, also IGI-ḫa-lum CT 32 10 ii 27; Ḫa-al-DINGIR PBS 11/1 46 ii 12, list; cf. ARMT 1 144 and 156 (Šunuḫraḫālu), also Bauer Die Ostkanaanäer 73a for WSem. personal names with the element ḫālu/ḫāli. Stamm Namengebung 286 n. 3.

ḫālu A v.; (1) to become liquid, dissolve, (2) to exude (a liquid), (3) ḫullu (uncert.); from OB on; I (iḫūl for mng. 1, iḫīl for mng. 2), II (uncert.); wr. syll. and SAL+ÁŠ; cf. ḫālu.

A.KAL = ḫa-a-[lu] Antagal C 266 (in group with záb[u], itat[tuku]); [ḫa-aš] SAL+ÁŠ = ḫa-lum Sᵇ I 334; tu-ḫa-la 5 R 45 K. 253 ii 19, gramm.

(1) to become liquid, dissolve: li-zu-ub li-ḫu-ur (error for ul) ù liḫ-[ḫarmit] may he flow away, dissolve and melt RB 59 pl. 8:27, OB lit.; ḫu (var. ḫu-ú)-la zūba itattuka dissolve, flow away, drip away drop by drop (said to waxen images) Maqlu I 140, also KAR 80 r. 23; kīma ṣalmī annûti i-ḫu-lu izūbu itattuku kaššāpu u kaššāptu li-ḫu-lu lizūbu littattuku as these images have dissolved, have flowed away, have dripped away drop by drop, (so) may the wizard and the witch dissolve, flow away, drip away drop by drop Maqlu II 146f., cf. PBS 1/2 133 r. 4; ina zābi ù ḫa-a-lu ū'a a'a iqtati napištuš (RN) ended his life woefully in hemorrhages (lit. in flowing away and dissolving) AAA 20 pl. 97:161 (p. 89), Asb.

(2) to exude (a liquid) — (a) in omen texts: šumma KI māti damī i-ḫi-il if the soil of the land exudes blood CT 39 13a:1, Alu; šumma KI māti damī i-ḫi-il-ma damūšu NU nu-uḫ-ḫu-ma [...] if the soil of the land exudes blood, and the blood cannot be stanched, and ... ibid. 7, also ibid. 13 (which adds la ik-kal-lu-ú-ma one cannot stop [it],

and ...), also ibid. 2–6 (with milk, honey, oil, naphtha and mucus [upāṭī] instead of blood), also CT 39 33:50 (with, instead of KI māti, KI É.DINGIR URU the soil in the temple of the city's god), also CT 40 47:16 (with A.ŠÀ A.GÀR a field in the [irrigation] district), also CT 29 48:12 (with KI-tim EN. LÍLᵏⁱ the region surrounding Nippur); [šumma KI] URU napṭa SAL+ÁŠ if the soil around the city exudes naphtha CT 39 10:26, Alu, cf. ibid. 18–25 (also with SAL+ÁŠ), also CT 39 13:1–13 (with i-ḫi-il instead of SAL+ÁŠ); ina ḪUL KI KUR ša damī i-[ḫi-lu] against the evil (portended by the fact that) the soil of the land exudes blood CT 41 23 ii 18, rel.; šumma Adad pīšu iddīma KI marta i-ḫi-il if there is a thunderclap, and then the soil oozes gall ACh Adad 3:21, cf. ibid. 33 (said of salt), also ibid. 4:35 (of oil), etc.

(b) in med.: [z] Ú. MEŠ-šu(!) enša lu damī i-ḫi-il-la (if) his teeth are weak (i. e., loose) or bleed (lit. exude blood) AMT 69 12:2, cf. AMT 28 2:3.

(3) ḫullu (uncert.): [...] ba. ta. lá. lá. e: [a-w]a-tam la iq-bu-ú tu-ḫa-a-li-iš-ši of a word that she did not say you .... her (tuḫāliši perhaps to be taken from e'ēlu and translated 'you accused her' cf. LÁ = ubburu, to accuse), but also ḫālu, "denouncer") RA 24 36 pt. 2:8, OB lit.; cf. 5 R 45 K. 253 ii 19, cited above.

ḫālu B v.; to tremble, shake; from MB on; I (iḫīl, iḫāl).

[mu.zu] ḫu.luḫ.ḫa an.na mu.un.pà.da ki.a ba.ab.ús.sa(!): šum-ki/gal-du ina AN-e i-za-kar-ma KI-tim i-ḫal he pronounces your awe-inspiring name in heaven and the earth shakes BA 10/1 100 No. 21:12.

(a) said of the earth, etc. (in lit.): ša ina rigim pīšu ... itarraru qerbētu i-ḫi-il-lu (var. i-ḫi-lu) ṣēru at whose thundering ... the fields tremble, the plain shakes Ebeling Handerhebung 98:21; ina tīb tāḫāzišu danni tupqāte ultanapšaqa i-ḫi-il-lu šadāni the ends of the world are in pain, the mountains quiver at his mighty onslaught in battle 3 R 7 i 9, Shalm. III, cf. šamû erṣetim ultanapšaqūma šadāni u tâmtum i-ḫi-il-lu Winckler Sammlung 2 1:5; ša ina tīb kakkēšu ezzūti [...] ušrabbūma i-ḫi-il-lu dadmū (the kings) at the onslaught

3

(handwritten notes at bottom:)
— small capitals, 6-point type = Kap. 6 pt
~~ capitals, 6-point type Roman = Kap. 6 pt each
— italics/cursive
‡ single space = Normaler Zwischenraum
‡ 1½ space = 1½ Zwischenraum
6-point type = 6 pt

SAMPLE PAGE. The Letter H, typeset 1955, with editorial remarks by Hallock.

AFTER H

THE CAD AND OTHER DICTIONARIES

The manuscript of the H volume, encased in a wooden casket, was sent off to the publisher in a parade organized by our friend Margaret Bell, executive secretary of the Oriental Institute, which wound its way, headed by Margaret blowing a toy trumpet, along the Institute's corridors. This rather childish exuberance was, unbeknownst to and unintended by the participants, construed as a sort of triumphal march and offended a number of the onlookers, whereas its sole purpose was to provide an outlet for the pent-up energies of the staff that had worked so intensely during the last weeks preceding the finish, during what came to be called "the endspurt."

With the appearance of Volume H, a crucial step had been taken: the actual publication of a volume of the CAD, for all its mistakes and awkwardnesses of presentation still the first step toward the realization of a project that had undergone many transformations since the 1930s. The impetus for this "bursting into print" (to use a phrase of our colleague Michael Rowton when referring to his own work) was, as already indicated, in no small measure given by the *Middle English Dictionary* (MED) concurrently in preparation in Ann Arbor. In later years, whenever Sherman Kuhn, the director of the MED project who succeeded Hans Kurath in 1962, and I exchanged notes at meetings of the Dictionary Society of North America, we found to our surprise that the two dictionaries progressed at an uncanny parallel pace. Upon Kuhn's retirement, Robert E. Lewis became editor-in-chief of the MED, and the project switched to computer composition as, to quote Richard Bailey of the University of Michigan and president of the Dictionary Society of North America, "the customized IBM electric typewriter golf balls drifted into history." While the MED was, though reluctantly, converted to hypertext mark-up language, the CAD, too far advanced to make the conversion painlessly, did not avail itself of

the new technology. For some attempts in that direction, see the
section on Computer Concordance.

Comparisons are difficult to make, but if we take as an example
the MED's longest letter, S, published in 18 fascicules with a total
of 1,268 pages and thus comparable to the CAD's Š, published in
three parts with a total of 1,365 pages,[86] it took the MED six years,
from 1986 to 1992, to produce it, and it took the CAD five years,
from 1981 to 1986, to prepare the manuscript and another six years
to see it through press.

It is perhaps less surprising that both the CAD and the MED
grossly underestimated the length of the completed dictionary. In
1956, the length of the completed MED was estimated at approximately 8,000 pages; in 1963 the estimate was raised to 10,000 pages;
in 1984, still under Kuhn's editorship, the estimate was 12,000, and
in the same year Editor-in-Chief Lewis estimated it at 13,000. The
1998 estimate was already 15,000, that is, almost double the original estimate. The projections of the CAD's length and timetable
were similarly unrealistic. "Breasted guessed that the final product
might run to about 3,000 pages in six volumes,"[87] and in 1949 Gelb
estimated it at 4,000 pages in three volumes,[88] "but the first fifteen
published volumes already include about 6,200 pages." [89] While I
don't know what caused the MED's underestimation, with the
CAD it was simply that the articles got longer, as more references
were quoted and more in extenso, more of them were translated
and not just marked "cf." The reason for this expansion was
twofold. One reason was the desire to supply the reader with more
material, both the non-Assyriologist reader who needed translations of the entire quote, and Assyriologists who did not have
access to the texts cited; this latter need was driven home to
Oppenheim when he found, upon teaching at the University of
California in Berkeley, that books cited in the CAD articles were not
available in the library of the university. Thus, it fell to the CAD to
include all the necessary data.

A testimony to the merit of this practice comes from a colleague
in Santa Barbara:

> At Yale and Chicago, it was quite easy to do the necessary work [scil., with
> cuneiform texts]; everything was at hand. Out here, it's quite difficult. So I've
> come to appreciate the CAD in a way I never did…a veritable extensive con-
> cordance (!) of material that I'd never be able to read otherwise. I'm grateful for
> the textual quotations.[90]

Scholars in other disciplines also praise the CAD's practice of
giving not only extensive quotes, but also full translations of them,
so that the nonspecialist is able to use the Assyrian Dictionary. This

aspect of the CAD of which I had not been aware was brought home to me by Anna Morpurgo Davies, the distinguished Indo-Europeanist of Oxford University, when she said that a dictionary of a language one does not know is mostly unusable, so she was surprised to see that she could use the CAD, because it has not only quotes, but also a full translation of the quotes. Moreover, an overview at the beginning of the article shows how it is structured.

The other reason for greater prolixity was the publication of von Soden's *Akkadisches Handwörterbuch* (AHw.), wherein it was found that sometimes AHw. managed to cram more information into the lemma in much less space than did the CAD.

To widen the field of comparison: The Berlin Egyptian Dictionary, on which the CAD was to be modeled, was initiated in 1897; the first of its five volumes appeared in 1926 (thirty years after the project was begun) and the last in 1931; it was itself modeled on the Thesaurus Linguae Latinae whose publication was initiated in 1894 and is not yet finished in 2002.[91]

More and more space was allotted to each entry in the MED too. As Editor-in-Chief Lewis described to me, the articles became more fulsome with time; while Kurath initially wanted only synonyms, as time went by the entries contained more citations and more translations. The reasons for this expansion may have been similar to those that prompted a like development in the CAD.

While the letter H was declared "the average size" letter, comprising 1/20 of the file cards in one filing cabinet, it would have been no surprise that the estimate was off the mark. So it was not without astonishment that the CAD staff saw that the guess proved correct. For example, the letter M occupied three filing cabinets and indeed its publication extended over two volumes (parts 1 and 2) of 441 and 324 pages, respectively; the letter Š, which filled five filing cabinets, needed three parts totaling 1,365 pages. All the while, however, the space devoted to individual words grew longer; similarly, it seems, AHw. too expanded its coverage, since the proportions between the two dictionaries did not change substantially.

EDITORIAL POLICIES

The original announcement (see p. 35) of the impending publication of H stated that "present plans are to publish at least one large volume a year, or two of smaller compass. Corrections and additions will be prepared continuously in the editorial office and will be issued, as sufficient material is assembled to make up a separate volume of supplements, from time to time." This plan necessitated, of course, that as soon as H was sent to the printer, work would concentrate on the volume next in line, in this instance moving backward in the alphabet, Volume 5 (G).

Indeed, G too bears the date 1956, no doubt owing to its smaller size—148 pages as against 266 of H—but also to the sustained "high" of the staff after the successful launching of H. The Assyriological and editorial staff remained the same, but the position of assistant to the editor was added, filled by Elizabeth Bowman. Miss Bowman eventually took over all the editorial tasks after the resignation of Hallock, who had been editorial secretary for Volumes H and G; she steered the CAD between Scylla and Charybdis for many years to come.

The layout of Volume G differs substantially from that of H and has set the pattern for all subsequent volumes. As Oppenheim's Foreword states, "The present volume of the CAD follows in general the pattern established in Vol. 6 (H). Only in minor points such as the organization of the semantic section, and especially in the layout of the printed text, have certain simplifications and improvements been introduced which are meant to facilitate the use of the book."

As editorial secretary, Hallock oversaw the English and strove for consistency in style and references. The "drafters" and editors often chafed at his editorial changes that in their eyes betrayed the nuances and the flavor of the original quote in order to conform to some ideal of correct English grammar and idiomatic English.[92] It was only under Hallock's successors that such conflict between the Assyriological staff, predominantly non-native speakers, and the editorial end of the enterprise was solved.

While Hallock still appears on the title page of Volume G (1956) as editorial secretary, the CAD had acquired, as mentioned, a sensitive and highly intelligent manuscript editor, Elizabeth Bowman, as assistant to the editor. I met her in 1953 at the summer Linguistic Institute at Indiana University and we remained friends while she went on to obtain a Ph.D. in English linguistics at the University of Chicago. She let herself be enticed into joining the project and remained with it for six years, from 1955 to 1962. She ruled it, as Oppenheim put it, with an iron hand, supervising the English as well as the style of abbreviations, quotes, and similar technical matters and overseeing typists and other lowly part-time workers. Even after she moved on, she wrote,

> ... I am still with the Assyrian Dictionary—I mean I empathize with its endeavor—in spirit, and would like to have a progress report. I suppose the

English language is again taking the beating from which I tried to rescue it while I was there.[93]

And:

> I suppose you are now sending back the second page proof for Ṣ and we will soon see the finished product. Remember to check the typefaces on the title pages—gosh, it will be funny to see a title page of the Assyrian Dictionary without my name on it—you've got to watch those Augustinians like a hawk. Let me know when Volume A/1 goes out.
>
> Now I never replied to Leo's kind offer of March 5 to take the errant child—me—back to the bosom of the Dictionary and let me reign again in Room 323. Really, there is nothing I would rather do. Every now and then I can't help thinking, "Life was so peaceful at the Dictionary." But I guess I must be one of these onward and upward types, ever striving, etc., to say nothing of the great improvement in salary here. Nevertheless, those were happy days, and a great deal was accomplished, even though my contribution was purely routine.[94]

Still, the age of experimentation did not seem to be over: Volume G included, at the end, a nine-page list of Additions and Corrections to Volume 6 (H). Fortunately for the project, this procedure caused so much hue and cry that it was abandoned forthwith.[95] Director Kraeling objects:

> We agreed before publishing H that any Addenda or Corrigenda were to follow at the end of the series. I admit that this is a long time. But I dislike the practice that developed unbeknown to me in Volume G to add them at the back of the next succeeding volume. They are bound to get lost back there since after some years no one will remember the order in which the volumes appeared and know where to look for addenda to a given previous volume. Consequently, I trust that before repeating the procedure in G we can have a talk about this in the plenum of the Editorial Board, or between you and me, to devise a plan on this subject that will make sense.... The Dictionary is intended and will be used as a Dictionary. It should *not* be used as a forum for the detailed presentation of the history of the project or of the procedure of the editorial operation. Such history could eventually be written for separate publication (in JNES as Thorkild suggests?) and copy sent gratis to all subscribers. I request that no decision on this matter, whether with reference to Volume A or to any other context, be taken without consultation with and the concurrence of the director of the Institute.[96]

Indeed, had the projected Additions and Corrections gone ahead, soon no one, not even the CAD staff, would have remembered whether to look for additions to E in Volume G or in Volume D, and so forth. As to Kraeling's second suggestion, about keeping "the history of the project or the procedure of the editorial operation" for a future publication, it is only now, with this essay, that Kraeling's suggestion is being fulfilled, in part.

LINGUISTICS AND LEXICOGRAPHY

Elizabeth Bowman, the assistant to the editor, was not the only member of the staff who was linguistically trained and inclined. I too had come to Assyriology from linguistics, although not the descriptive linguistics then in vogue in the United States, and this background was perhaps a factor in my being hired in 1952 by Gelb. Gelb himself was a champion of the then current structural linguistics approach and had close friendships and many discussions with his linguist friends Eric P. Hamp, Robert B. Lees, and George Bobrinskoy. The early 1950s were still dominated by post-Bloomfieldian structural linguistics, the pre-Chomsky, neatly-laid-out theory that appealed to Gelb's sense of order and symmetry. His SOP was built, he maintained proudly, on linguistic principles, and he did not see how his colleagues could not instantly have been won over by it. Gelb regularly encouraged his students in Akkadian to take at least one course in the department of linguistics. For me he arranged a fellowship to attend the Linguistic Institute at Indiana University in the summer of 1953, where I not so much learned philosophies and techniques (that were anyway soon to be superseded by new developments, beginning with Chomsky's pathbreaking 1957 book *Syntactic Structures*), as made long-lasting friendships that accompanied me throughout my career at the University of Chicago. A special boon of the Institute was forming a friendship with Elizabeth Bowman and thereby securing an outstanding manuscript editor for the CAD. When the Linguistic Institute was held at the University of Chicago in summer 1954, at Gelb's urging Oppenheim and Rowton also participated along with me in a seminar on lexicography given by W. Freeman Twaddell of Yale University.

My personal research was for many years divided between philological (text-critical) and linguistic studies. The latter bore fruit in my monographs on *The Elamite Language* and *A Linguistic Analysis of Akkadian*.[97] I also served as spokesperson for the CAD toward the linguistic community, at meetings of the Dictionary Society of North America, and in a paper given at a Conference on English Bilingual Dictionaries in 1969, published in *The Linguistic Reporter* of the same year.[98] It is even likely that my proclivities had an influence on the CAD's practices, which in the area of transcribing Akkadian words had already diverged, under Landsberger's influence, from the commonly accepted practice.

My monograph on the Elamite language (which eventually earned me my tenure) turned out to be one of the causes for dissension among the editors. Gelb, although he was the one who invited me, feared that Hallock, to whom he was bound by a long-standing friendship, would be eclipsed by me in the field of Elamite that both of us studied, and was reluctant to support my promotion until Hallock was named professor of Elamite.

Other causes for disagreement reflected inherent differences in the interpretation of the source material as well as in the tactical approach to lexicography. Jacobsen agreed with Oppenheim in the beginning against the dilatory attitude of Gelb and supported the plans for publication. He had an enduring relationship with Landsberger until his resignation from the Board. Landsberger, understanding Jacobsen's concerns, while complaining about the "insane haste" that prevented him from probing the depths of the meanings, also knew that the project must move forward; at every crucial juncture he resolutely joined a united front with Oppenheim and me and came to the CAD's defense, even as he knew the risk of losing Jacobsen's friendship and companionship.

The epistemological differences underlying the compilation of the Dictionary had never been formulated, explicitly or not, nor had the necessity for formulating them even been acknowledged. (The SOP dealt mainly with formal matters.) Especially divisive was the matter of the speed of production. Speed was crucial for Oppenheim, who believed that it was essential to show the Assyriological world that the Dictionary could be produced and that a slackening of momentum would doom the project. Conversely, any speed, be it minimal, was always too high for Landsberger, who needed to familiarize himself with the word's environment and entire family. He needed time to immerse himself in the culture-historical aspects or material culture aspects of the word he was working on—and he was increasingly asked to work on precisely such words—and chafed under the deadlines Oppenheim tried to impose.

Landsberger's comments, written longhand on yellow foolscap with a no. 3 pencil, so that they were always difficult to read, encompassed the word's semantic family and other derivatives or semantic parallels. Still, he did not mind if all his remarks could not be incorporated in the pertinent Dictionary article; these remarks, however, were not discarded or forgotten—rather, the "yellow sheets" were xeroxed (in an effort to preserve them) and then filed under the word or words that were extensively discussed in them. As an example, Landsberger's "yellow" written on the occasion of the adverb *minde*, in which he discussed several of the adverbs meaning "perhaps," was used in the redaction of the articles *surri* (*assurri*) and *tuša*, when attention was drawn to Landsberger's treatment of these adverbs through a filecard that simply said "See BL's yellow under minde."

A corollary to the question of speed was that of depth. As mentioned, Landsberger delved deeply into the meanings and usages of the word treated and its etymological and semantic family, so that "depth" for him was not one-dimensional; whereas Jacobsen tried to tease out meanings by successive probings ever deeper into a word's hidden layers. It is in this way that the questions of speed versus depth plagued the Editorial Board.

Vast areas remained undefined or were interpreted according to the individual editor's convictions and preferences. Such items as the preferred and proportional lengths of articles remained unspecified, without weighting assigned to say verbs over nouns, earlier attested versus late words, material objects versus concepts, and the like; often one or the other editor, displaying a special interest in a word, gave it disproportionate space. Thus, it came about that one of the outside readers, himself a specialist in religious texts, who had been sent the manuscript of Volume G, could ask: "Who is so interested in *gurgurru?*"—the word *gurgurru*, defined in the CAD as 'a craftsman working in wood and metal', having taken up substantial space of the volume. In fact, it takes up four and a half columns of the printed Volume G, versus 21 lines, sub *qurqurru* 'Metallarbeiter, Kupferschmied', in AHw., and two lines, *qurqurru* 'metalworker, esp. coppersmith', in the *Concise Dictionary of Akkadian.*

This "metalworker" also serves as an example for pinpointing other differences in scholarly outlook that affected the collaborative efforts of the editors and staff. For Gelb, socioeconomic history reflected and "explained" the ancient civilizations far better than their literary and religious history, a dichotomy that he expressed succinctly as "Tammuz and onions." His belief is also evident from his 1952 report on collecting material for the CAD:

> ...in the academic year 1951–1952, we are supposed to finish gathering all the sources and ordering the files. I should estimate that we have collected up to now [in four years] over nine-tenths of all the Akkadian sources. That includes such large groups as royal-historical inscriptions, economic-administrative texts, letters, epics and legends, laws, Amarna, Cappadocian, Susa, Mari, Nuzi materials, all gathered completely. The rest of the literary, religious, lexical, medical, mathematical, and astrological-astronomical texts, as well as the remaining commentaries, omina, oracles, and rituals, will be taken care of this year.[99]

With the exception of the category "epics and legends," the "nine-tenths" of the sources are all of the "onions" variety. The core of the Mesopotamian tradition and the entire scientific literature, what Oppenheim called the "stream of tradition" texts, those that were used to train and formed the curriculum of the Mesopotamian scribes and were collected and deposited in the royal archives of Assur and Nineveh, could, according to Gelb, be incorporated in the files in a single year. In effect, the corpus of literary and religious texts, and such scientific texts as divination, medicine, and astrology, exceeds, with its close to two hundred thousand lines, the Homeric epics and the Old and New Testaments taken together.[100]

In contradistinction Jacobsen, who had a more speculative bent, attached great importance to such matters as fertility cults and the king's annual sexual union with the goddess—the so-called *hieros gamos*—to secure the fertility and prosperity of the land, and extrapolated his theories from mainly Sumerian sources that may not have had relevance to the "Assyrian" Dictionary. His theories were sometimes referred to by Oppenheim, uncharitably, as a "pinpoint horizon." However, once they were expressed in his *Treasures of Darkness*,[101] they were inspirational for many Sumerologists.

Nor was the CAD supposed to be a vehicle for the ideas of one individual. The editors of the CAD were not to engage in proselytizing. For Oppenheim, the CAD was not a means to proclaim some truth, only "to make an orderly though not always definitive presentation of the accumulated material," as he had stated at the outset. For Jacobsen, however, it was important that his insights into the grammar of Akkadian—some of which were considered faulty by Landsberger[102]—and especially his ideas about Mesopotamian religion (see above p. 40)—find their way under appropriate entries in the Dictionary.

Differences arose on more lowly, technical levels too. In the matter of transliterating cuneiform texts, the CAD adhered to the system advocated by Gelb, although there were always minor deviations in the treatment of Sumerograms, that is, Sumerian words embedded in the Akkadian text but that were to be read in Akkadian. Less well systematized was the matter of transcription of Akkadian words, especially the use of diacritical marks to indicate length of vowels. The notation of vowel length as a distinguishing feature in the grammar of Akkadian did not follow the standard Akkadian grammar;[103] in February 1955, Hallock described a system based, he said, on "arbitrary principles" that he had devised for use in the CAD, but it was never published. The CAD's practice was eventually set out in 1965, post factum, by our colleague J. A. Brinkman, who also pointed out the many inconsistencies in the various volumes.[104]

Oppenheim could very well live with such ad hoc, or as some would say haphazard, decisions as long as the spirit of the enterprise was intact and the momentum did not slacken. Gelb's withdrawal, even though caused by other reasons, spared him the anguish of being associated with inconsistent editorial practices.

THE CAD'S FATE IN THE BALANCE

The peaceful collaboration on the Dictionary did not last very long. Whereas Gelb slowly adjusted to the new style of the CAD and was pleased to be consulted on individual words and points, relations with Jacobsen took a turn for the worse. In October 1958 he challenged Oppenheim to abide by the agreements entered among the editors of the CAD.[105] On October 28, 1958, Oppenheim wrote to Jacobsen in answer to Jacobsen's eight-and-a-half pages long letter written two days earlier. In his letter Oppenheim answers "formally the question contained in the final phrase of your letter that it is and always has been my intention to 'exercise my duties in conformity with the legal framework which has been properly proposed and accepted'....I am also willing, as I have always been, to accept any positive criticism of my work as editor in charge, but I shall not answer your 'accusations' nor retort with a display of my achievements..." Jacobsen acknowledged it on October 30, with the words, "I very much appreciate your unhesitating and clear statement of your commitment to the legal framework of the Dictionary and your firm statement of intention to operate within it."

Still, the intervention of Director Kraeling became necessary to set the ground rules. In November 1958 he laid out the organizational principle of the CAD:

> May I use this opportunity to set forth briefly my understanding of the working of the Dictionary staff. The Dictionary staff is, in my judgment, fortunately and appropriately organized so as to have both a Board of Editors and an editor-in-charge. The Dictionary is a group enterprise of the Institute and the group has a head. As in the workings of the Institute there is democracy and there is leadership. We avoid the pitfalls of autocracy and the vague impersonal operation of committee.
>
> The Board and the editor-in-charge each have their responsibilities and prerogatives. The Board as a whole is charged with formulating policy, and its several members with participation in the actual preparation of the text of the Dictionary according to individual competences. All members of the Board should see and have an opportunity to comment upon and criticize the articles of the Dictionary before they go to press, provided of course that they are available to do this during a reasonable period of time. The editor-in-charge is the administrative and executive head of the enterprise, and to him the Board has

delegated the right to make the final decisions as to how the materials are to be organized and as to what comments and corrections proposed shall be incorporated in the articles. Naturally the editor-in-charge will act responsibly as a scholar in weighing the comments made and changes proposed, but unless he has the final say as to what is to be printed there can be no homogeneity in the product nor can it be guaranteed that there ever will be a product.

It is the necessary corollary of the prerogative and responsibility of the editor-in-charge that he be ready to "take" the criticisms, justified and unjustified, of his decisions. The Board and the editor-in-charge have the common assurance that if they have acted to the best of their ability and insight within the sphere of their own particular responsibility and prerogative, the product of their labors will merit the praise of those who understand the limits of all human endeavor. We need not fear the comments of the self-constituted perfectionists.[106]

Details of the disagreements that arose in the fall of 1958 and that had necessitated the intervention of Director Kraeling are not available. The reason, or perhaps only the excuse, for them may have been the question of my own reappointment or promotion. I had at that time been research associate with parenthetical rank of assistant professor since July 1, 1956. When the question of my promotion was brought up by Kraeling, in a letter to Oppenheim sent from the east coast where he was convalescing, Oppenheim wrote a glowing letter to Kraeling dated October 24, 1958, recommending promotion to associate professor with tenure; the promotion was supported by Eric P. Hamp of the department of linguistics on the basis of his evaluation of my analysis of the Elamite language in *Handbuch der Orientalistik*.

Under other circumstances, I would have been willing to accept reappointment as assistant professor and wait for the promotion to associate professor with tenure, but in view of the deteriorating situation of the CAD I indicated to Director Kraeling that I could not accept reappointment as assistant professor because "[i]n the last few days, a situation arose which, considered from my personal point of view, gives me an uneasy feeling about my future career with the Institute." I feared that I could not feel "assured that the Assyrian Dictionary Project was going to continue without such an interruption which would terminate my appointment with the Institute."

Ironically, it was the appointment of a junior member of the team that led to an at least temporary respite in the dissensions surrounding the CAD, instigated by Jacobsen's real or perceived dissatisfaction.

The chain of events started with an invitation received by Oppenheim from Johns Hopkins University. Director Kraeling convened a meeting of the Editorial Board on March 5, 1959, to inform them of Oppenheim's wishes were he to agree to stay in Chicago. Oppenheim had stated to Kraeling, "If I am to stay it will be because of the hope that by devoting virtually all the rest of my scholarly life to the Dictionary I can accomplish more than if I were to devote myself to a variety of enterprises. For this I need the proper working conditions."[107] At that meeting, by majority vote, the members of the Editorial Board designated Oppenheim editor-in-charge for three years beyond June 30, 1960[108] and director of the Assyrian Dictionary Project. Jacobsen, in protest, resigned from the Editorial Board, but his resignation was not accepted by the director at that time.

Mindful of his colleagues' perception of his role, Oppenheim also made clear to Kraeling that

> Shouldered as I am with the responsibility of seeing that the manuscript of the individual volumes actually goes to press and that the proofs are read, I am by force of circumstances placed in the position where I seem to be the one who pushes everybody around and where I seem to be requiring of people hasty and immature judgments. I think my colleagues on the Board should realize that if any part of the Dictionary is ever to appear there must inevitably be an end to any period of reflection and reconsideration and that to determine it is one of my functions.[109]

In consequence, on March 25, 1959, Oppenheim presented a memorandum on the Assyrian Dictionary to his colleagues. It states, among other things:

> As my colleagues well know, I have discussed all decisions, minor and major, with each of them, alone or in groups, in that direct and informal way which is my nature and which I feel I must insist upon. The exchange of carefully styled letters full of innuendos, etc., kills mutual trust just as does the mise-en-scene of official meetings. The formal meeting of acceptance of each volume should, of course, continue as agreed upon.
>
> There is nothing in the setup of the Project that would not permit any one of the editors to take over the editorship of one or more volumes of the CAD. If the other editors agree on this, allot time and personnel, and if this editor agrees to dedicate all his time and effort to such a volume, the Project can only profit by such an arrangement.

Also in March, I too received an invitation, to wit as lecturer in the department of Semitic languages at Harvard University. The director convened the tenured voting members of the Oriental Institute on March 31 "to consider what to recommend" in regard to this offer. In the absence of other records of the two meetings, these momentous events of March are best recounted in the words of Kraeling, in a letter addressed to Jacobsen, and in a memorandum to the voting members.

In his letter to Jacobsen, Kraeling writes:

Your description of what has transpired since March 13 is in my judgment inaccurate, incomplete and unsatisfactory.... After the distress of the past weeks it is necessary that more peaceable conditions prevail in the Dictionary group so that work may be resumed. We must have an end, therefore, of memoranda, meetings and the regurgitation of past events. It is important to remember in this connection that the editors of the Dictionary have the first claim on Professor Landsberger's time for the furtherance of their work.[110]

Kraeling maintains, in his memorandum:

I think we saved the Dictionary, even if we left Thorkild [Jacobsen] aggrieved ...I hoped that time would heal the wounds and that eventually, like Jay [Gelb], he would make his adjustment. This hope was blasted in connection with the final episode of 1958–59 when the tenure appointees among the voting members gathered in this office [March 31, 1959] to consider what to recommend apropos of the invitation that had come to Erica to accept an appointment at Harvard. This was the occasion at which Thorkild publicly accused Benno and Hans [Güterbock] of having "rigged" the invitation because of the way they had replied to an inquiry from Harvard. Everyone was incensed. My feeling was that Thorkild had effectively cut himself off from the Dictionary group by this statement. Therefore on the next day I accepted his resignation from the Board.[111]

Jacobsen himself, in a letter to the members of the Assyrian Dictionary staff, justified his resignation by invoking as reason "that recent events have tended to concentrate all effective power in the hand of the editor-in-charge and have rendered the system of checks and balances hitherto prevailing inoperative." He also reaffirmed his conviction that "the announced policy of the Dictionary ... must be interpreted so as to permit a reasonable degree of penetration and in a few special cases even maximal penetration" and that "actual power of decision in Dictionary matters should lie with the board as a whole rather than with any single person."[112]

While Jacobsen's criticisms were ostensibly based on the legal framework of the Dictionary's "constitution," he also acted as champion for Landsberger, since he considered Landsberger was not given enough time to study the drafts submitted to him—drafts that he discussed with Jacobsen every afternoon—so that they were taken away before he could give them sufficient attention, the "maximal penetration" alluded to in Jacobsen's letter. A deeper cause for friction was, as mentioned, the refusal of the CAD to include Jacobsen's speculative interpretations of some core religious terms. Several of these terms occurred in Volume E that was sent to press in the end without waiting for Jacobsen's comments. During the time that Jacobsen would have devoted to reading the manuscript of Volume E, he was occupied by a project he had undertaken for the government of Iraq, a project for which, by the way, both Rowton and I supplied Akkadian textual material, and spent much of the year 1957 in Iraq.

When Oppenheim sent off the volume without waiting for Jacobsen's comments, this act provoked Jacobsen's no doubt long-simmering resentment. He prepared a list of mistakes in the E volume and, at a meeting of the voting members of the Oriental Institute on November 17, 1959,[113] accused, not me and Oppenheim, but Director Kraeling with dereliction of duty for his "inability to maintain the scholarly standards of the Institute," declaring that "he had lost all confidence in the Director." Such a maneuver, aimed at discrediting us as unfit to run the CAD but taking the form of an attack not on us two Assyriologists but on the director of the Oriental Institute, was typical of Jacobsen's modus operandi. Nevertheless, he proposed a vote of confidence in the director, with some corollaries that were meant to place restrictions on the editor of the Dictionary. The voting members, however, refused to take a vote that included such corollaries.[114]

The history of the events is described by Carl Kraeling in a memo to the voting members of the Oriental Institute prepared on December 9, 1959. In eleven typewritten pages he gives a detailed account of Jacobsen's statements and his—the director's—role in finding a solution to the Dictionary problem. (The memo appears as Appendix 7.) Kraeling's valiant defense of the project and the scholars involved in it saved the Dictionary—at least temporarily—but led to his resignation.

Kraeling, among other statements, asks the voting members:

> ...if after having heard the statements on both sides you were convinced that there had been dereliction of duty on the part of the director in his relation to the Dictionary project or that the continuance of the present procedure for editing and publishing the Dictionary was not desirable or both, you would so indicate by additional actions, as is your perfect right to do.... What happened to Thorkild [Jacobsen] in this connection was only what Jay [Gelb] had gone through in 1954 when another similar disagreement developed that caused his resignation as "the Editor" of the Dictionary.
>
> ...There was a perfectly valid agreement drawn up in 1952 by which Jay as "the editor" of the Dictionary was charged with the responsibility of setting up the systematic presentation of the articles and in which Benno [Landsberger] was charged with a special redevelopment in depth of such articles as could profitably be so developed. Then in 1954 the group decided it could not accept Jay's conception of the way the articles should be written. The matter was not settled by "persuasion or freely accepted compromise" of which Thorkild's statement and your action of November 20th speak. Jay was neither persuaded nor did he accept compromise; he did what Thorkild did, he resigned, only he did not suggest that the director, who attended the painful session in which it all

happened, had been guilty of it all and hence derelict in his duty.... Jay was deeply hurt and refused to participate actively in the work of the first volume of the Dictionary now put in the hands of Leo. I discussed policy in this matter...and our decision was to try to let time heal the wounds. It did take time but Jay, I am happy to say, did make the adjustment...his help was being asked for and was appreciated. But the basic fact is that Jay disappeared from the active workers of the Dictionary...

The next development inside the Board was Thorkild's non-availability...I...recall that whenever the matter of Thorkild's taking on other commitments came up I queried him about their effect upon his Dictionary work.... A serious lag in the arrival of this [namely, the Sumerian] material could very well drive an "editor in charge" to despair. Something like this seems to have happened in connection with Thorkild's Diyala enterprise, from which time the estrangement between Thorkild and Leo became more marked and as the result of which the effective editorial staff was reduced to Benno, Leo and—in a junior capacity—of Erica.

...I made a special trip from the east coast (November 1958) partly to help as best as I could. The occasion was a memorandum from Thorkild to Leo freighted with barbs and seeming to imply as did also his statement of November 17th to you that over against the "great Olympians" editors in charge and directors are choreboys. We managed to keep the ship afloat through that episode, but then came the invitation to Leo to move to Johns Hopkins, an enviable and excellent offer for him, one that serves to show how much greater was the esteem in which Leo was held outside of Chicago than by Thorkild, a fact which may have aggravated Thorkild's disturbed mental state.[115]

In December 1959, Oppenheim addressed a written statement to the voting members in response to the personal attack on him and Director Kraeling by Jacobsen. He stated:

His support at the outset of my editorship, I may even say his enthusiastic support when, in 1956, I was appointed editor-in-charge in one of the customary, recurrent crisis situations, is a matter of record. At that time I made it clear that (1) I consider the Project a finite affair, and (2) that the work has to be done by a staff genuinely interested in it. Nothing illustrates better the change in mood and scholarly interest of the staff than the fact that in these last five years, in which the myth of the perfect file collection and of the smoothly working organization has been destroyed, more books and articles on assyriological topics were written by the staff than by former collaborators in any corresponding period of time. Which also goes to prove—to anyone open to reason—that the "nervous pace" and terrific pressure exist only in the minds of those who just do not want to face the facts that a) to write a dictionary means to stick out one's neck; b) that there are no "interesting" or "important" words for the lexicographer but just—words; and c) that it is much more difficult to elucidate the meaning of a specific word than to utter trite generalities... I am well aware that I have not been the only target of Dr. Jacobsen's zeal to improve, broaden, deepen and penetrate scholarly thinking. His past record of resignations speaks for itself, unless one assumes that all the various bodies with which Dr. Jacobsen found it impossible to cooperate consisted of undemocratic, incompetent and dishonest individuals.... Evidently he regards it as inexcusable that I have, in my tyrannical, undemocratic way, tried to raise the level of cooperation on the Dictionary Project from one of uninterested subordinate drudgery to one of enthusiastic devotion, with the full right to questions and criticisms recognized for all participants.[116]

What Oppenheim perceived as the aims and duties of the lexicographer bears a surprising similarity to the statements made by James Barr, for a time Godfrey R. Driver's successor as editor of the *Oxford Hebrew Lexicon*, at a meeting of the Society for Biblical Literature in 1985,[117] the most memorable of which in my mind is that "the dictionary does not get written except by writing it."[118] And Oppenheim's attitude toward the Dictionary staff, as described in his statement, was indeed one of generosity, not unlike the attitude of Michael Polanyi who professed that the only way to teach is by example.

In the autumn of 1960, Jacobsen produced a paper titled "Spot-check on the CAD volume 7." The paper was intended to demonstrate the grievous faults found in the printed volume I/J to support his contention that the CAD was run by incompetent people.[119] By that time Kraeling had resigned from the directorship of the Institute, notwithstanding the "vote of confidence" proposed by Jacobsen, and the eminent Egyptologist John A. Wilson, who had served as director from 1936 to 1946, was appointed acting director.

Wilson, an honest and scrupulous man, asked Landsberger to evaluate the criticisms of Jacobsen. In reply, Landsberger submitted on January 25, 1961, "An Opinion of Quality, Value, and the Future of the CAD" of seven typewritten pages, followed by a "Critical Evaluation of CAD and AHw" of twenty typewritten pages. [120] While Landsberger tried to treat Jacobsen's criticisms tactfully, acknowledging some of his criticisms as justified but considering them of minor importance, he never hesitated to acknowledge the importance and value of the CAD and its staff; he was in particular supportive of Oppenheim and me, who had been the target of Jacobsen's attack. He declared to Jacobsen: "I have felt justified in protecting two people—not from attack or constructive criticism, but from a threat of extinction of a worthwhile project to which they have truly devoted a great portion of their life's efforts.... I cannot but suspect that you move not sine ira et studio, but rather that the truth lies in the embers of a quarrel which was originally not concerned with the project itself."[121] In the days and months that followed he tried to persuade Jacobsen to return to the Editorial Board, but to no avail. [122]

So Volume 7 (I/J) was published by an Editorial Board of three, and so were the next two volumes, Z and Ṣ. In 1964, my name was added to the Board. Not only the editors changed; so did, subtly, the substance of the Dictionary too, as Kraeling recognized in September 1960:

> I was happy to have also all the news about the third floor and then more recently the volume I/J of the Dictionary, another stone added to the great structure that Leo and you [Reiner] are rearing so effectively. Yes, I read around in it for my own amusement enjoying particularly the postscripts to some of the articles that seemed to qualify the content of the articles themselves. I suppose that in a way this represents Leo and Benno, refusing to close the books on a given subject. But it is not a bad idea. It makes the reader feel that all this is an emerging thing, not a monument of what the Germans call Klassizismus.[123]

John Wilson left the interim directorship after one year, having stated that "The director of the Oriental Institute feels it necessary and important that he cast his vote of confidence in the present editor-in-charge and the present associate editor. With them in responsibility CAD may continue production; without them it is highly doubtful whether production could continue."[124] The appointment of a new director was made difficult by Jacobsen's opposition to the appointment of Robert McC. Adams, the candidate favored by most. Thus, for another year the Institute had to be run by an acting director, this time through recalling from retirement the respected Emery T. Filbey, who was known for his expert handling of many delicate situations.

In spite of Wilson's vote of confidence in the editor-in-charge and the associate editor, the unimpeded advance of the CAD had to depend on the next director.

In spring 1962, the president of the University asked Jacobsen to chair a new committee for the directorship. In a letter to the members of the Institute, Jacobsen enumerated the qualifications necessary for the position, and revealed the committee's recommendations to the president of two scholars (Rodney Young and Frank Cross) who

> were voted acceptable candidates by the voting membership with large majorities. In addition, the name of John L. Caskey, of Cincinnati, has been discussed in the committee and the committeee unanimously recommends it as its preferred candidate. The name of Robert M. Adams has been informally proposed by several members of the Institute. The committee values Mr. Adams very highly as a person and colleague but does not think that he meets the requirements stated above. While this view is shared by other members there is also a group that considers Mr. Adams fully qualified and supports his candidacy strongly.

Obviously, some members of the Institute had found it necessary and expedient to approach the president directly. Hence, a second letter from Jacobsen, dated the same day, says that "the name of Robert M. Adams has been informally proposed by several members of the Institute who have spoken to the president in its favor. Since it is the task of the committee to ascertain the preferences of the members, we ask you to evaluate this name with the others in your ranking."[125]

Moreover, the fabric of the Dictionary was again threatening to come apart as I received—for a second time—an invitation to Harvard, this time as full professor with commensurate salary. The temptation was great, but I thought I would remain at Chicago if the future of the Assyrian Dictionary Project could, at last, be assured. Oppenheim took this opportunity to present the case to Edward Levi, then provost of the University, who realized that the future of the Dictionary depended on the appointment of the next director of the Oriental Institute.

When Oppenheim took me along to see Levi, upon hearing that I had received an offer from Harvard, he said in his usual deadpan way, "Everybody had an invitation to Harvard," and upon hearing that the present offer from Harvard was my second one, said, "Everybody who is somebody has had two invitations to Harvard." Naturally he was aware of the situation in the Oriental Institute and proceeded to appoint Adams who took over the directorship in May 1962, and I turned down the Harvard offer. Thereupon Harvard offered the professorship to Jacobsen, who immediately accepted. Thus, sadly, ended a relationship that could have been productive and would have enriched the Dictionary and provided continuing friendship and company to Landsberger.

In reviewing the situation as incoming director, Adams sought independent opinion about the standing and the future of the Assyrian Dictionary, although he personally believed in its current leadership and organization. He set these out lucidly in a memo to Provost Edward Levi.

> The views of Mr. Ephraim Speiser are particularly pertinent…for they come from a man for whom the respect of all his colleagues here was apparent during the search for a director for the Oriental Institute. Mr. Speiser informs me that ideally he would be inclined to favor Jacobsen's view of what the Dictionary should be. But he believes that no Dictionary would be able in practice to fulfill this vision. He states categorically that the importance to scholarship of the CAD volumes that have appeared is immense…"Whatever you do," he urged me over the telephone, "take no decision that will jeopardize or delay the appearance of the CAD."
>
> The complexity of the undertaking is such that any set of volumes produced by a limited number of individuals will reflect the scholarly strengths and weaknesses of its authors and will be subject to criticism from others. In other words, the existence of errors or uneven coverage may be an argument for

enlarging the size of the project to take account of a wider range of scholarly competence but it does not thereby justify a substantial alteration of the circumstances under which production of an urgently needed Dictionary has actually gotten underway.... This does not mean, of course, that no improvements are possible, but merely that improvements should be sought under the general authority and initiative of Mr. Oppenheim as editor-in-chief.[126]

He also pointed to the essential role of the University's recognition of the project when he said in the same memo, "Clearly, one of the strongest forces operating to keep [Miss Reiner] here has been the recognition by the administration of the importance of the Dictionary Project and the support which the administration has repeatedly extended to its staff."

Until his death in 1968, Landsberger loyally supported the Assyrian Dictionary in spite of his sorrow at losing Jacobsen's human and scholarly companionship. Under the title "Progress in Assyriology," in a lecture delivered at the meeting of the American Oriental Society on April 14, 1965, that has remained unpublished apart from a short excerpt in *Orientalia,* he stated:

> It goes without saying that the greatest progress in Assyriology has been attained by the two competing dictionaries.[127]...[the CAD] differs from other projects still to be mentioned; it differs in this way: it does not postpone the final action indefinitely or leave decision for the next generation; it ignores almost frivolously[128] both systematization and specialization; it is neither deterred nor frustrated. In short, it is *an adventure of great dimension* with both the dangers and the unexpected findings of an adventure."[129]

THOSE WHO DRIFTED FROM THE COURSE

The recounting of the struggles of the CAD Project to attain the status and the equilibrium that made its survival possible and that has so far occupied much of this narrative must not, of course, pass over those dedicated and essential scholars who furthered, at one time or another, the CAD's progress and growth, although they veered away from its course to pursue other projects. An account of the CAD should especially dwell on the figure of I. J. (Jay) Gelb, whose creative role has been acknowledged several times in this account.

Gelb had a tremendous energy that he channeled into the reorganizaton of the CAD. In his personal research he was often pioneering, such as in his work on "Hieroglyphic Hittite, " and ventured into domains not many Assyriologists were interested in or even knew about. Through his connections to and friendships with colleagues in linguistics—at the time structural linguistics—he analyzed Old Akkadian, especially its writing system, from a linguistic point of view; he also insisted that his students take at least one course of Introduction to Linguistics. His own contribution in this area was his *Study of Writing*.[130] With the advent of the computer age, he was among the first to take advantage of the possibilities inherent in this medium, and produced (with the help of R. M. Whiting and others) a *Computer-aided Analysis of Amorite*.[131]

It is unfortunate that Gelb, who was instrumental in the revitalization of the CAD, chose to dissociate himself from the project for reasons that are not well understood and that hurt him and the project as well. Still, in spite of his (temporary) withdrawal from the Editorial Board, he remained available for consultation and I like to think pleased when he was consulted about Old Akkadian or some point of grammar. Oppenheim, as editor-in-charge, always encouraged the younger staff members to go to Gelb for advice.

He was curious and interested in many things; he loved to discover and was surprised to find that others had made the same discovery before him. If somebody else knew something that he had just discovered, he was apt to ask, How do you know? He was very kind to students and young people and loved to teach, not only students, but also colleagues who attended weekly seminars in his office. In fact, he urged his students—and colleagues, whenever possible—to take classes in linguistics (at that time, Bloomfieldian structural linguistics). It is only proper that his name remain listed among the members of the Editorial Board on the title page of the CAD.

Another recruit for the reorganization of the CAD who did not last out the stretch was Michael B. Rowton. Nevertheless, his work is incorporated not only in the early volumes of the CAD (A, B, E, G, H) but also in Volume S that appeared in 1986, long after his retirement. Rowton came to Assyriology after a varied career in business and in the military. He became interested in the Near East when he was stationed as an officer in army intelligence in the Middle East during World War II. After the war, he took up the study of ancient history and Assyriology, first with W. von Soden in Germany, where he served as a member of the occupation control commission in the British Zone, and then with Georges Dossin in Liège. His wife, whom he married in England, was of Hungarian extraction, and they arrived in Chicago with a charming and well-mannered young boy who seemed the living image of Little Lord Fauntleroy to Rowton's American colleagues.

He was invited to join the CAD by Gelb in 1952 and arrived at the same time as I did. A mature man but being of a modest character, Rowton listened to the criticism and advice of his colleagues good-naturedly. He contributed many manuscripts in draft to the volumes of the CAD, but it was obvious to his colleagues that his main interests did not lie in lexicography, but rather in Akkadian grammar and especially in ancient history. Thus, he was slowly detached from writing CAD drafts and, from about 1964 until his retirement in 1975, allowed to immerse himself in the study of dimorphism and nomadism. He was working on assembling his individual studies into a book when he suddenly died on January 9, 1986.[132]

A DOZEN YEARS OF PROGRESS AND PEACE

After Adams's appointment as director of the Oriental Institute, there followed a period of twelve years free from the dissensions that had used up much time and energy, years productive for the CAD as well as for Oppenheim personally. They saw the publication of his *Ancient Mesopotamia* (1964), *Glass and Glassmaking* (1970), and many substantial articles, in addition to the publication of the letters A (two volumes), B, K, and L, and sending to press M (two volumes), bringing the total to fourteen volumes, covering thirteen letters, that is, thirteen of the twenty-three characters of the Latin alphabet used in transcribing Akkadian. All the while Oppenheim, anticipating his retirement, groomed me as his successor, having realized from early on that my presence on the staff provided continuity. With the death of Landsberger in 1968, there gradually evolved a procedure by which the senior advice and final decision on CAD manuscripts was deferred to Oppenheim while I did the actual editing on manuscripts prepared by both the junior staff and by Oppenheim himself.

By writing large sections of each volume, organizing the presentation of lexical items, interpreting cuneiform texts of all genres and periods, and, not least, by his insight into the complexity of Mesopotamian civilization as expressed in the written records, Oppenheim assured the progress and quality of the CAD. He had the knack of reducing a seemingly unmanageable pile of filecards to a closely argued and logical edifice, what he had called, in the Preface to Volume H, an "orderly though not always definitive presentation of the accumulated material." He concentrated on the long and difficult words and left more and more of the details of editing the basic manuscript for content and organization to me. As an example, of the words in the large volume 8 (K), published in 1971, Oppenheim wrote 60% while Biggs and Renger each wrote 15%, and Sweet and Weisberg the remaining 10%.

Research assistants or research associates continued to work on the CAD; in addition to the pioneers Hirsch and Kienast, several came from the ranks of Chicago graduates (Brinkman, Caplice,

FIGURE 4. Editor-in-charge Oppenheim with Associate editor Reiner.

Harris, Leichty), others from various American or European universities. Among the latter, Biggs, Hunger, and Renger attained faculty status and stayed on; others (Grayson, Shaffer, Stol, Weisberg) left to occupy chairs of Assyriology at other institutions but remained faithful consultants for the CAD.

During these years, and even in Landsberger's lifetime, questions of matters Sumerian were increasingly submitted to Miguel Civil, who was originally invited in 1963 as assistant to Landsberger in the preparation for publication of the lexical series *Materials for the Sumerian Lexicon* and in 1965 joined the Oriental Institute faculty representing Sumerology. His contributions to the Dictionary in the field of Sumerian and in various technological matters were soon recognized as essential, and he was invited to join the Editorial Board in 1967. He is listed as member of the Editorial Board on the title page of Volume A, Part 2, published in 1968.

Meanwhile, of course, the collecting of material continued. New cuneiform publications were excerpted by the Assyriologists, and indexes of words in various books and journals were cut up and pasted on cards by student-assistants and clerical staff. The exact number of cards in the files was based on estimates; in 1955 they were thought to number one million, and that number kept increasing. As for the number of quotations—full citations as well as references to sources—we had recourse to Civil's interest in these matters. In 1970 he made the following estimates:

estimated number of references per average (300 pp.) volume: 15,000
actual number of references for 11 volumes (A–K, Ṣ and Z, 3,730 pp.): 165,052.

The estimated number of references in Volume R (441 pp.), published in 1999, is 20,000, still in keeping with the 1970 estimates.

Satisfied that I could take over the running of the project, and in the knowledge that Civil would provide needed advice, Oppenheim stayed on for one year after his retirement in 1972, and in 1973, after I had taken over as editor-in-charge, moved to Berkeley, California. However, he agreed to spend two months in the fall and two in the spring in Chicago, during which time he would continue to write Dictionary articles. This arrangement worked for the academic year 1973–74 but was torn asunder with Oppenheim's sudden death in July 1974.

FIGURE 5. Filing Cabinets (Hunger, Reiner).

AN EPILOGUE TO THE STORY

Oppenheim's death occasioned a profound change in the life of the project as well as in my own relation to it. Gone was the reassurance that I could always save questions until Oppenheim's return to Chicago, or if necessary consult him by mail or telephone. The CAD had lost a collaborator who had planned to write the long and "difficult" words. No other senior Assyriologist was on hand to turn to when I needed advice. The attitudes of the members of the CAD staff were varied: Some, possibly resenting that a woman was in charge, offered to take on "editing" themselves but their initiative soon petered out. At this juncture the importance of the contributions of Miguel Civil, not only in the field of Sumerian, but also in various other matters, became evident. Civil's interests in and knowledge of material culture and technology matched Oppenheim's, and his expertise assured the quality of the Dictionary in these fields after Oppenheim's death. In these difficult days of transition I increasingly turned to him for advice and support so essential for the continuation of the project.

A new wave of research associates[133] signed up to work on the CAD to help me run the Project. They comprised both old friends—colleagues who had worked on the CAD earlier, such as Caplice, Kienast, and Renger—and new recruits. Of these, the seasoned, mature scholars who held professorial rank at other universities, such as Dietz Edzard, Hermann Hunger, Joachim Oelsner, Simo Parpola, and Klaas Veenhof, were able to leave their home institutions for a few months to write dictionary articles; Hans Hirsch, another of the early collaborators, volunteered to take over the editing of a volume. A few mid-career scholars (van Soldt, Stolper, Wiggermann) also came for visits of less than a year. Appointments of young research associates (Astakhishvili, Black, Gallery, Groneberg, Jas, Ludwig, Rochberg, Joan G. Westenholz) continued; their one-year appointments were often extended to a second year.

Nevertheless, the reduction in the permanent staff and a change in priorities contributed to the slowdown so well predicted by Oppenheim. Still, under my own editorship (1973–1996), nine more

FIGURE 6. The Dictionary Room in the 1970s (Veenhof, Gallery, Hirsch).

volumes, covering the six letters N, Q, R, S, Š, and T, were sent to press. Of these, seven volumes appeared, while two (R and T) were delayed at the printer's, owing to difficulties that arose in J. J. Augustin's firm.

When in 1979 a recent Ph.D. from the University of Pennsylvania, Martha T. Roth, joined the project as research associate, it soon became clear that here was no transient visitor; in 1980 she joined the faculty of the Oriental Institute and the Department of Near Eastern Languages and Civilizations "with primary responsibility to the CAD" as her contract stated; so did, in the same year at a more senior level, Matthew W. Stolper, who had previously come to Chicago in 1978 as a visiting CAD staff member. Roth's publications and ongoing work on the laws and legal procedures in Babylonia complemented the Dictionary staff's specialization; clearly, her talent and her dedication to the project boded well for the future. When I recognized Roth's potential, I did what Oppenheim did on my behalf: I began to groom her as my successor. In 1996 I was able to step down as editor-in-charge in the knowledge that the CAD would be in able and dedicated hands. Indeed, under Roth's editorship (1996–), one of the two volumes delayed at Augustin's (Volume R) finally came out in 1999, published by Eisenbrauns, which has taken over the printing of the CAD, and another volume, P, was sent to press. In 2002, only four volumes covering five letters remain outstanding: the long-delayed Volume T, Volume P in press, and Ṭ and U/W to be published.

A subtle change has occurred in the overall character of the CAD, as its editors changed. During the Oppenheim era the organization of the articles, and especially the discussion at the end, often contained speculative arguments about the institution to which the word referred, and these arose and were fostered and fed by anthropological and sociological concerns well known and of interest to Oppenheim. With Landsberger on board, such wide-ranging discussions branched out into a variety of subdisciplines, especially history and history of the language family. The value of these speculations was recognized by Kraeling in his above-cited letter:

> ...the postscripts to some of the articles [that] seemed to qualify the content of the articles themselves. I suppose that in a way this represents Leo and Benno, refusing to close the books on a given subject. But it is not a bad idea. It makes the reader feel that all this is an emerging thing, not a monument of what the Germans call Klassizismus.[134]

FIGURE 7. Editor-in-charge Reiner with manuscript editor Daniels.

Under my own editorship, since my interests and formation were not primarily anthropological, discussions became more formalized. Of course, if one of the drafters brought in comparative material from outside Assyriology it was always welcomed, but the CAD's wide range narrowed considerably; its place was taken, more and more, by grammatical considerations, reflecting the interest and competence of outside consultants, and the emphasis on "grammatical correctness" was reinforced by some of the reviews that singled out some unfortunate mistakes. In retrospect, there is no doubt in my mind that the criticisms of Jacobsen and his accusations of my and Oppenheim's "ignorance of elementary grammar" had, at least as far as I was concerned, a paralyzing effect. The "reflections about the establishing of meanings" deemed so essential by Landsberger in 1961[135] tapered off for lack of time, lack of interest on the part of the editors on the Board, and occasionally lack of courage of the editor-in-charge.

Even so, every new word still brings a new excitement and challenge, and the resident staff as well as the visitor take up with great gusto the task of establishing the meaning of a seemingly well-known word in all its nuances. In this fashion, a word written for a particular volume may end up as a small monograph on an institution or practice, such as, for example, the word for "king" (šarru) or for a type of pledge (titennu).

More than thirty years after Kraeling's just-cited comment, a member of the staff characterized the Dictionary in a similar way:

> The criticism that the Dictionary provokes is incorporated into later volumes in the form of reconsideration, rebuttal, amendment or mere changes of emphasis. Furthermore, to an ever-growing degree, collaborators on the Dictionary have had their basic understanding of the language and the issues of interpreting it shaped by the Dictionary itself from their earliest professional training…Now,…after a career of vigorous debate with the Assyriological community, [the Dictionary] has some of the characteristics of an eminent senior scholar: set, sometimes old-fashioned ways of expression, coupled with such attributes of maturity as an immensely complex and subtle understanding of the material and its interrelationship, constant reflection and reevaluation, leading sometimes to refinement of older views, sometimes to acknowledgment of uncertainty, and often to wholly new insights about the words, the texts that carry the words and the historical moments that produced the texts.[136]

Work on the CAD also served as incentive for creative work outside the Dictionary. Goaded by the often inadequate filecards and the need for searching further where the filecards gave out, the staff, and the visiting collaborators as well, were prompted to delve into one or another aspect of Assyro-Babylonian civilization. This personal, individual research resulted in an impressive number of articles and books, beside, and in addition to, the collaborators' full-time work on the CAD. The pressure to produce did not come from outside; it was generated in the environment of the CAD and the example set by the working habits of its senior staff: Landsberger, Oppenheim, and Gelb.

The CAD has served as model and encouragement for similar long-term enterprises, and in addition sent out into the Assyriological world a goodly number of young scholars. Some of these scholars now are nearing or in retirement; they, and some younger ones as well, bear the stamp of their association with the CAD. They have learned that the understanding of the whole—the whole text, the whole context, the whole genre, the whole civilization—is more important than the exact meaning of some detail; they have seen respected senior scholars admit that they do not know something, that there are things they do not understand at the moment, and that it is no shame not to know provided one is willing to learn. I believe they are fortunate to have had the opportunity to work in that "intellectual atmosphere characteristic of the 'Third Floor' of the Oriental Institute where the CAD took root and found its own identity." [137]

THE ASSYRIAN DICTIONARY AND
THE OUTSIDE WORLD

The preceding account dealt with the internal relationships that shaped the CAD and with the circumstances and personalities that led to the revival, reorganization, and maturing of the project, centered in the Oriental Institute. It was in the Institute that the various crises erupted and were not so much solved as papered over or given ad hoc solutions. But from the beginning, the Project had, and maintained throughout its history, the international character that was considered essential from the outset. First manifested in the collaboration of nonresident Assyriologists who prepared text editions and filecards, continued through the agreement coordinating the publications of the "short dictionary" prepared in Germany and of the CAD, it endures to this day through the financial contributions of the Union Académique Internationale.

The CAD's relations with the outside world—be they scholars or institutions—are briefly sketched in the following sections.

COLLABORATORS

The visiting collaborators brought to Chicago from 1947 (Armas Salonen and Jørgen Laessøe) to 1952 (J. R. Kupper and J. V. Kinnier Wilson) by I. J. Gelb as part of his reorganization of the CAD normally spent one year on the project, while the two junior staff members (Reiner and Rowton) hired in 1952 were expected to be integrated into the team for a longer term and indeed eventually obtained faculty rank. Oppenheim, too, upon taking over in November 1954 and realizing the importance of the infusion of fresh blood, strove to increase the scope of expertise by inviting younger scholars to work on the project, especially after the death of F. W. Geers—who in his quiet way contributed a great deal to the identification and understanding of the literary material—in January 1955,[138] and of A. Heidel, who had spent the last years of his life in the Near East, in June 1955. At first, Oppenheim assigned work on Volume D to a freshly graduated student of his, Rivkah

Harris, who was in part supported by a grant from the American Philosophical Society, and on Volume I/J to William L. Moran, at the time on leave from the Pontifical Biblical Institute in Rome.

Moreover, it was thought to be helpful if all words beginning with a sibilant were treated at the same time, so as to sort out the voiced, voiceless, and emphatic sibilant initials, Z, S, and Ṣ. These three letters were to be treated simultaneously, by different drafters. Oppenheim looked for young talent abroad and in 1957 invited Burkhart Kienast, a young German scholar who came from the school of the great Sumerologist Adam Falkenstein in Heidelberg. Kienast, now professor emeritus from the University of Freiburg, has been the CAD's most faithful supporter since 1958, returning to work on various volumes over a span of forty years, beginning with Volume Z, up to and including Volume Ṭ (not yet published). Z, by Kienast, was published in 1961 with a Foreword dated 1960. Ṣ, also by Kienast, with the collaboration of Rivkah Harris and R. F. G. Sweet, was published in 1962, with a Foreword dated October 1961. S was also begun, by Michael Rowton, but it was eventually abandoned when Rowton's interest veered in other directions; it was taken up again only in 1979, by R. I. Caplice; its Foreword is dated February 1981, and the publication date is 1984.

The resident staff included, in addition to the members of the Editorial Board, in the 1960s the faculty members Biggs, Reiner, Renger, and Rowton. They were responsible for the basic preparation (writing the manuscript on the basis of the filecards) and their ranks were usually augmented by the visiting research associate. For editing the basic manuscript for content and organization, I assumed increasing responsibility.

The University of Chicago supported the CAD project from its beginnings in the 1920s throughout its history, most of that time from University resources. Salaries of faculty and staff were always borne by the University of Chicago; in the postwar years, up to eight Assyriologists were employed at any one time on the CAD; their number was drastically reduced in the 1970s when retired or resigned faculty were not replaced. The faculty on the CAD staff usually had a lighter teaching load, but the Landsberger-Oppenheim generation worked ceaselessly throughout the four quarters of the academic year with only a brief vacation here and there. Their scholarly research was accomplished evenings and weekends, and still their contributions equal and surpass in quantity and quality those of most scholars, their contemporaries. Today, few projects generate that level of commitment, and the CAD is no exception, even though it is still buoyed by the accomplishments of past generations and by the prospect of the nearness of the end. If such projects as the CAD are not undertaken any longer, it is because of the anachronism of the *travail de bénédictin*—a work of lonely, laborious, patient scholarship, characteristic of Benedictine monks—needed to accomplish it. While such work is replaced, so they say, by electronic resources, to my mind we are back precisely at the *travail de bénédictin*, because in spite of the networking and the media the scholar still works alone. In fact, he or she works in greater isolation than when such a collective enterprise was carried out by a team of dedicated and self-selected scholars.

The financial situation at the University of Chicago and the prevailing trend of applying for government support for scholarly projects eventually forced the CAD to prepare grant proposals to support the Dictionary. The University continued to fund the salaries of the faculty, in fact a greatly reduced faculty, after the retirement of Rowton in 1975, the retirement and shortly thereafter the death of Oppenheim in 1974, and the resignation of Renger in 1976. The CAD was fortunate to receive funds from the National Endowment for the Humanities beginning in 1976 though often on a matching basis; to raise the matching funds became increasingly difficult as time went on. Of the junior scholars invited to the project, several (Biggs, Renger, and Hunger) were retained as regular faculty, and each brought to the project his own expertise but could hardly replace in knowledge, wisdom, and dedication the scholars of the founding generation.

As I wrote to the director of the Institute in 1974, after the death of Oppenheim:

> ...What we lack is a scholar of the intellectual capacity, range of interest, and creative ability that Landsberger and Oppenheim represented in our midst. It is difficult for a project like the CAD to continually transcend the daily routine without such stimulation, and to continue to be in the forefront of interpreting Akkadian texts and culture at the same high quality level. For the sake of this high intellectual quality I would always rather put up, though not gladly, with occasional sloppiness in reference citations, a minor fault that can be easily corrected by the reader. [139]

THE CAD AND VON SODEN'S *AKKADISCHES HANDWÖRTERBUCH*

While the CAD continued working backward, on E and D, which were published in 1958 and 1959, respectively, von Soden's *Akkadisches Handwörterbuch* (AHw.) began to appear; the first fascicle, a to ašium, appeared in 1959. The AHw. gave the CAD a means to gauge its own progress and coverage. In fact, the only letter produced independently by the two projects is the letter D; for E (and the following letters G, H, I, J, as well as Ṣ and Z), AHw. could make use of the CAD, while the CAD could profit from von Soden's A, B, and the letters following H (that is, K, L, M, N, P, Q, R, S, Š, T, Ṭ, U/W, but not I, J, Ṣ or Z). The coverage and accuracy of the letter E in each dictionary became crucial, because CAD E provided the foundation of the criticisms by Jacobsen and von Soden's E was scrutinized by me to establish whether AHw. was above criticism (it was not). My assessments of AHw.'s letter E were not published but were used by Landsberger in his "Critical Evaluation of CAD and AHw" (see above p. 59). Most of the time, however, the dictionaries engaged in polite disagreement when warranted. Just as AHw. corrected any mistakes found under the corresponding entry in the CAD, so the CAD, upon the advice of A. Sachs, listed at the end of its article any error that was found in the AHw. entry, and expunged, by listing it with two asterisks, entries in AHw. that were non-existent in the language. This latter procedure replaced the corrections to entries in Bezold Glossar that had been practiced in Volumes H (e. g., **habratu), G (e. g., **gitmuru), E (e. g., **erku), D (e. g., **dušahu), I (e. g., **išrubū), Z (e. g., **zanzirad), and Ṣ (e. g., ** ṣamū), which preceded the publication of AHw.

Eventually, the numbers of the pages devoted in AHw. to each letter not yet published in the CAD were listed on the blackboard in Room 319 (the office of the editor-in-charge) and that list remained there for many years until an officious janitor cleaned the blackboard. It was a relief to see that Volumes P and S were about of equal length, and R slightly shorter; that T was of a standard size, but Ṭ much shorter. For Martha T. Roth, current editor-in-charge of the CAD, the small size of AHw.'s Ṭ and the fact that of the sole remaining letters to be published, U and W, a large part was included in previous volumes under A and M,[140] are a great relief and comfort.

COMPUTER CONCORDANCE

There was a time when using computers for the CAD was considered. In the 1960s an attempt was made to interest the faculty of the humanities in the possibilities offered by the University's computing facilities. Oppenheim and I had a meeting with Professor

Robert Ashenhurst, at the time associate director of the Institute for Computer Research, to discuss the feasibility of putting the Dictionary files into electronic format. Two points were against it. First, at that time the system was still rather primitive and encoding the filecards would have been a very cumbersome process. Second, Ashenhurst said this would be a three-year project, and Oppenheim feared precious time would be squandered on the conversion. As he put it: "I don't have three years to waste."[141]

Nevertheless, various experiments with data processing had been started. In 1961, Oppenheim started looking into the possibility of setting up a procedure for creating a reference index to the CAD that would be compiled for each volume as it appeared and finally published as a supplement volume to the completed CAD. One of the CAD's secretaries, Doris Weil, had access to computer programming and initiated the project; negotiations were taken up later with the newly established Computation Center of the University of Chicago in 1965, and a pilot test project was authorized by the Institute's Director Adams in 1966.

Volume B (2) was selected to test the feasibility of a computer-generated reference index of Akkadian texts quoted in the CAD. Originally the reference index was meant to direct the reader of a cuneiform text to the translation offered in the appropriate volume and page of the Dictionary, but it could—and did—serve to delight students who could compare the sometimes widely divergent translations of the same passage given under different headings.

This project was conceived in the early 1960s when the technology was not sufficiently advanced. The procedure proved to be too cumbersome: First, each reference in the printed volume was underlined by an Assyriologist, in red or green according to whether the quote was translated or cited without translation. The underlined references were then transferred by a secretary to specially designed cards. The cards, in turn, were entered on code sheets in accordance with the Computation Center's instructions. From the code sheets Barbara Hudgins, an experienced typist who had previously worked for the CAD, produced punchcards on a rented keypunch machine. Finally, the punchcards were sent to the Computation Center that eventually produced a printout.

After the printout for Volume B was produced, the project was abandoned. It was too time-consuming and costly, and the procedure involved too many steps at which errors could creep in, so that the result contained too many errors. Another problem became evident when the sample printout was produced: The citations in the CAD were not uniform (and, I should add, they still are not), and the same cuneiform text may have been, and often was, cited from different sources, so the entries under a particular source were incomplete. Moreover, the fact that the entries had to be right-justified to keep the references in correct numerical sequence had been overlooked . We also soon realized that in subsequent volumes new editions of many texts were to be cited, and the reference index would be inconsistent and in some cases obsolete.

In addition to this experiment of a reference index, two other indexes, on filecards, were initiated: an English-Akkadian index that excerpted the Dictionary Volumes A to K and Ṣ and Z;[142] and an index of Sumerograms, begun by R. T. Hallock but not continued after him. Both these indexes may eventually be compiled with the help of the computer once the last volume of the CAD is published.

OUTSIDE READERS

While writing drafts of Dictionary articles has involved, from the start, an international crew, Oppenheim wanted to broaden the input by submitting the edited articles, in manuscript or at the galley stage, to outside readers. Our first and most faithful reader was, as mentioned, W. G. Lambert, who made his comments on the unchecked manuscript.

Galley proofs were sent at first to such former members of the Chicago staff as Professor Hans Hirsch of the University of Vienna, who had been a research associate early on, in 1960–1961 (and who returned for one year in 1978–1979); Hirsch, whose Ph.D. dissertation had been on texts from the Old Assyrian period, commented mainly on the Old Babylonian and Old Assyrian texts quoted; his keen sense for Akkadian grammar often queried, usually rightly, transcriptions and/or translations of literary texts too. The difficulty of Old Assyrian texts lies not in their language, though they were written usually by the businessmen who traded in Anatolia and not by professional scribes and therefore contain many idiosyncrasies of orthography, but in the nature of their subject matter, as they involve complex business transactions often described in abbreviated form or—for obvious reasons—by allusion only. Such texts can be understood only by those who are familiar with the parties and the transactions involved; thus Landsberger was able to a certain extent to "decode" the Old Assyrian texts for the Dictionary.

After Landsberger's death in 1968, Mogens Trolle Larsen, now professor at the University of Copenhagen and director of its

Carsten Niebuhr Institute of Near Eastern Studies, who had spent the academic year 1967–1968 at the Oriental Institute and who had specialized in these Old Assyrian texts, volunteered to check the accuracy of the Old Assyrian material in the CAD. For many years he made minor and often major corrections; his corrections were always perfectly founded and assured. I well remember how we had to rewrite the article *kārum*, which in the Old Assyrian texts is the term for the Anatolian trading colony, even though it was in galley proof already. "This just won't do," wrote Larsen, and proceeded to reorganize the Old Assyrian references. We of course capitulated, and the article was much improved.

After several years, Larsen had to give up commenting on the CAD galleys; we were fortunate that Klaas Veenhof, of the University of Leiden, the Netherlands, was willing to take over his role, and he is still our authority on Old Assyrian, as well as on other matters of his specialty.

Hirsch himself withdrew from reading CAD galleys in the late 1970s, but the practice of enlisting the help of outside readers has been kept up by other scholars with different specialties, different emphases. In addition to Veenhof's reading, galleys are read by Simo Parpola of the University of Helsinki, Finland, formerly a faculty member at the University of Chicago, with special attention to Neo-Assyrian.

A different type of reading has been provided, at a different stage of the CAD, by our most faithful reader, critic, and contributor, W. G. Lambert, until recently of the University of Birmingham, U.K. Lambert's teaching career began on this continent: first at the University of Toronto, and later at Johns Hopkins University, before he was appointed to the chair at the University of Birmingham. While in America, Lambert often came to Chicago to consult various textual sources and to read the CAD in manuscript. In the process he was able to suggest corrections and add unpublished references from his vast collection of literary texts. He continued to read the unchecked and uncorrected typescript of the CAD after his return to England, from the carbon copy—nowadays the photocopy—mailed to him.

Lambert's contributions are twofold: First, he has copied and collated a great many texts in the British Museum, so he can correct readings that were based on inaccurate copies and complete partially incomplete passages from his collection of fragments rejoined to previously published texts; he also can add significant new references to those cited in the dictionary manuscript. Second, his vast experience in Babylonian literary texts enables him to suggest readings and translations that the Dictionary had not considered (but that the editor-in-charge does not necessarily accept). Lambert's contributions come at a stage when they can be evaluated before the manuscript goes to press, thus avoiding the cost of changes in galley proof. The sting of Lambert's sometimes caustic comments is often tempered by his wit and humor, and it is impossible to hold a grudge against him even when, on occasion, his criticism does not seem justified.

NOTES

[1] E. M. Uhlenbeck, "Roman Jakobson and Dutch Linguistics," *Roman Jakobson: Echoes of his Scholarship*, D. Armstrong and C. H. van Schoneveld, eds. Lisse: Peter de Ridder Press, 1977, p. 485.

[2] See, for example, Robert L. Brown's comment: "As the foundations of scholarly truths become shaky with the realization that objectivity in research is impossible, it has become important to understand the methods, motivations, and intentions of those who write scholarly works." *Journal of the American Oriental Society* 115 (1995) 502.

[3] H. W. F. Saggs, *The Might that was Assyria*. London: Sidgwick&Jackson, 1984.

[4] Mogens T. Larsen, *The Conquest of Assyria*. London and New York: Routledge, 1996.

[5] Sally C. Humphreys, personal communication.

[6] A. L. Oppenheim, *Journal of Near Eastern Studies* 25 (1966) 144.

[7] I. J. Gelb, Introduction, Chicago Assyrian Dictionary, vol. 1 (A) part 1. Chicago: Oriental Institute, and J. J. Augustin, Glückstadt, Germany, 1964, p. vii.

[8] In his *The Oriental Institute*, Breasted evokes "the great Murray dictionary of the English language, at Oxford" (p. 383).

[9] J. H. Breasted, *The Oriental Institute*, Chicago: University of Chicago Press, 1933, 383–387.

[10] Benno Landsberger, paper read at the annual meeting of the American Oriental Society, April 14, 1965.

[11] Erman, Adolf and Hermann Grapow, *Wörterbuch der Aegyptischen Sprache*. 5 vols. Leipzig: J. C. Hinrich, 1926–1931.

[12] A. Leo Oppenheim, *Ancient Mesopotamia. Portrait of a Dead Civilization*. Chicago: University of Chicago Press, 1964.

[13] Oppenheim to Director John A. Wilson, January 28, 1961. No criticism of Wolfram von Soden's great achievement, the *Akkadisches Handwörterbuch*, was intended by this comparison, based only on the differences in organization and principles of coverage. In fact, Oppenheim acknowledged the CAD's indebtedness to von Soden in the Foreword, dated June 7, 1963, to Volume A of the CAD.

[14] *Evolution after Darwin: the University of Chicago Centennial*, Sol Tax, ed. Chicago: University of Chicago Press, 1960.

[15] *City Invincible*, Carl H. Kraeling and Robert M. Adams, eds. Chicago: University of Chicago Press, 1960.

[16] "Die 'City Invincible' makes good reading vor dem Einschlafen. Sie informiert über die Geisteshaltung dieses Landes. Einer der Erfolge des inzwischen abgedankten Direktors Kraeling war das sogenannte Symposion und dieses Buch: beide zusammen haben einige 10,000 Dollar gekostet. Das Geld ist von Rockefeller gespendet worden, der damit ein Seitenstück zu des verstorbenen Anthropologen Redfield (oft zitiert in O.I.) Projekt 'Urbanization' in die Welt setzte. Letzteres hat gegen Hunderttausend Subvention von Ford bekommen. Dagegen kann hier kein

Geld aufgetrieben werden, ein nicht populäres Buch zu drucken." (Landsberger to Fritz Rudolf Kraus, February 18, 1961.)

[17] "Oft, ja fast immer, ist unsere Lexikographie verkappte Kulturgeschichte, wenn auch kein andrer soweit gehen wird wie Jacobsen, nämlich ein ganzes Buch (trotz erbitterter Fehde darüber von mir als wertvoll anerkannt) über awīlum zu schreiben." (Letter of Landsberger to Kraus, December 9, 1953.) Landsberger refers to Jacobsen's draft of the word awīlum 'man', a draft of 100 manuscript pages that would have proved impossible to bring within the parameters of a dictionary article, had Jacobsen meanwhile not severed his connection with the CAD. This draft was repeatedly used as argument for the impossibility of running the CAD according to Jacobsen's views. The CAD entry amīlu covers nine printed pages.

[18] See section on "Collaborators," p. 75ff.

[19] "In dem Leser Ihrer Rede muss unbedingt der Eindruck entstehen, dass in dem künftigen Lexicon die Bedeutungen der akkadischen Wörter zu finden sein werden. Aber diese Ermittelung geht in den meisten Fällen über unsere Kräfte; es ist wahr dass wenn ich sehr intensiv daran arbeiten würde, vielleicht manche Bedeutungen herauskommen könnten. Ich sehe ab von obscuren Pflanzen etc,. wenn ich feststelle, dass für 60 % der akk. Wörter die Bedeutungen unbekannt sind und dass es auch gar nicht in der Zielsetzung des Dict. liegt, sie zu bestimmen. Sollte Gelb die Allein-Leitung wieder in die Hand bekommen und seine Sklaven finden, so wird das Dict. ein reines (und schlechtes!) Wortregister. Mit uns, L. und O. weniger, ohne uns, L. und O. mehr, ist das Dict. nur ein der nächsten Generation in die Hand gegebenes Mittel, die Bedeutungen zu finden." (Landsberger to Kraus, December 9, 1953.)

[20] The differences in their approach were set out in Landsberger's evaluation of the CAD made in 1961 at the request of Director John A. Wilson.

[21] A Concise Dictionary of Akkadian (SANTAG, vol. 5). Jeremy Black, Andrew George, and Nicholas Postgate, eds. Wiesbaden: Harrassowitz, 1999.

[22] "While in many ways we have consciously imitated the organization, procedure, and format of our sister dictionary, the Chicago Assyrian Dictionary (CAD), the much smaller size of the Hittite text corpus insures that the CHD [Chicago Hittite Dictionary] will be more limited in size and scope." The Hittite Dictionary of the Oriental Institute of the University of Chicago, vol. 3, Fascicle 1. Chicago: Oriental Institute, 1980, p. xv; "…the Chicago Assyrian Dictionary, whose pioneering work in Cuneiform philology serves as a model and foundation for the Sumerian Dictionary." Å. W. Sjöberg, The Sumerian Dictionary, vol. 2 (B). Philadelphia: The University Museum, 1984, Foreword, p. vi.

[23] City Invincible, p. 95.

[24] LSS NF 1: A. Falkenstein, Die Haupttypen der sumerischen Beschwörung. Leipzig, 1931; NF 2: W. Kunstmann, Die babylonische Gebetsbeschwörung. Leipzig, 1932.

[25] B. Landsberger, Der kultische Kalender der Babylonier und Assyrer. Erste Hälfte. LSS 6/1–2. Leipzig, 1915.

[26] By Walther Sallaberger's treatment of the Ur III calendar, in Der kultische Kalender der Ur III-Zeit (Untersuchungen zur Assyriologie und vorderasiatischen Archäologie, vol. 7). Berlin /New York: Walter de Gruyter, 1993.

[27] Samʿal, Studien zur Entdeckung der Ruinenstaette Karatepe. (Türk Tarih Kurumu. Yayınları. ser. 7; no. 16). Ankara, 1948; Brief des Bischofs von Esagila an König Asarhaddon (Mededelingen der Koninklijke Nederlandse Akademie van Wetenschappen, Afd. Letterkunde. Nieuwe Reeks–Deel 28–No. 6). Amsterdam, 1965; The Date Palm and its By-products according to the Cuneiform Sources (Archiv für Orientforschung, Beiheft 17). Graz, 1967.

[28] For example, "Assyrische Königsliste und 'Dunkles Zeitalter'," *Journal of Cuneiform Studies* 8 (1954) 31–73; 106–133, reissued as a small monograph; "Jahreszeiten im Sumerisch-Akkadischen," *Journal of Near Eastern Studies* 8 (1949) 248–297.

[29] "aus meiner Bossert-Rezension ist ein Buch geworden." (Landsberger to Kraus, May 16, 1947.)

[30] "'Früh' und 'spät'." *Archiv für Orientforschung* 3 (1926) 164ff.

[31] Immanuel Löw, *Die Flora der Juden*, vols. I–IV. Vienna: Kohut Foundation, 1923–1933.

[32] He referred to Gene Gragg's analysis of the "Syntax of the Copula in Sumerian," eventually published in *The Verb 'BE' and its Synonyms*, Foundations of Language, Supp. Ser., 8 (1968) 86–109.

[33] W. von Soden, *Grundriss der akkadischen Grammatik* (Acta Orientalia, vol. 33). Rome: Pontifical Biblical Institute, 1952.

[34] B. Landsberger, *Die Fauna des alten Mesopotamien nach der 14. Tafel der Serie HAR-RA = hubullu, unter Mitwirkung von I. Krumbiegel*. Leipzig: S. Hirzel, 1934.

[35] "Frivolously" stands for intended "recklessly."

[36] A. L. Oppenheim, "In memoriam Benno Landsberger," *Orientalia* NS 37 (1968) 367–370.

[37] Hermann Hunger, *Astrological Reports to Assyrian Kings* (State Archives of Assyria, VIII). Helsinki: Helsinki University Press, 1992.

[38] *The Interpretation of Dreams in the Ancient Near East. With a Translation of an Assyrian Dream-book.* (Philadelphia: Transactions of the American Philosophical Society, NS 46/3), 1956; *Glass and Glassmaking in Ancient Mesopotamia. An Edition of the Cuneiform Texts Which Contain Instructions for Glassmakers.* Corning: Corning Museum of Glass, 1970; *Cuneiform Texts from Babylonian Tablets in the British Museum*, Parts 55–57, Neo-Babylonian and Achaemenid Economic Texts by T. G. Pinches. London: British Museum Publications, 1982 (prepared for publication, according to the Foreword, by I. L. Finkel. The advertisement of the volumes by the British Museum Publications nevertheless states "by T. G. Pinches, edited by I. L. Finkel").

[39] "The Position of the Intellectual in Mesopotamian Society," *Daedalus—Journal of the American Academy of Arts and Sciences* (1975) 37–46.

[40] "On an Operational Device in Mesopotamian Bureaucracy," *Journal of Near Eastern Studies* 18 (1959) 121–128.

[41] Memorial tribute, delivered January 22, 1975, excerpts published in *The University of Chicago Record*, IX:4 (September 21, 1975) 135.

[42] Chiera's letter (March 2, 1932) was written soon after the Dictionary moved, along with the other projects of the Oriental Institute, to its new home from Haskell Hall, where it had been housed since its inception in 1921 under its first director, D.D. Luckenbill. For the early history of the Dictionary, see J. H. Breasted, *The Oriental Institute*, pp. 378–400.

[43] *Orientalia* NS 18 (1949) 376f.

[44] *Orientalia* NS 21 (1952) 358f.

[45] "An undertaking of the magnitude of the CAD is built upon the labor of a large number of scholars, but this volume owes a special expression of gratitude to Ignace J. Gelb of the Editorial Board. His reorganization of the Project in 1947 terminated a protracted state of semi-animation and changed decisively the nature of the CAD. Without the work executed under his direction the publication of the dictionary could not have begun."

[46] Cited, after Bacon, by Gelb, in "Lexicography, Lexicology, and the Akkadian Dictionary," in *Estructuralismo e historia: miscelánea homenaje a André Martinet*, vol. II (Biblioteca filológica, Diego Catalán, ed.), 63–75. Tenerife: Universidad de La Laguna, 1957.

[47] In a memorandum to John A. Wilson, director of the Oriental Institute, November 19, 1946.

[48] See Gelb, CAD A [volume 1 part 1] p. xvii. The agreement is described, and its original German wording quoted, in a memo of I. J. Gelb dated October 2, 1950.

[49] The Marburg agreement was given up in October 1954; Gelb resigned as editor-in-charge at the end of 1954. Nevertheless, his name is included among the members of the editorial board for Volume H (1956) and subsequent volumes.

[50] Gelb, *Orientalia* NS 21 (1952) 358.

[51] "Oppenheim ist übrigens ein gutmütiger Bursche, der sich selbst mit seiner Schluderei en gros nicht so wichtig nimmt. Sein assyriologisches Wissen ist immens. Er hat sich sofort als mein Helfer in praktischen Dingen angetragen und bewährt sich glänzend." (Letter of December 23, 1948.)

[52] "Er [Oppenheim] ist ein Mann von rührender Gutmütigkeit, lässt nie eine meiner classes aus, soll sich auch nach allgemeiner Auffassung in seinen letzten Publikationen radikal gebessert haben." (Letter of March 5, 1950.)

[53] "obgleich ich überzeugt bin, dass bei dieser Zusammensetzung des lexicographischen Generalstabs das Lexicon nur als verschlechterter Bezold herauskommen kann, muss ich diese Chance wahrnehmen … Das richtige akkadische Lexicon wird natürlich von Soden liefern." (Landsberger to Kraus, October 8, 1949.)

[54] Ich schreibe mir ein neues.

[55] Carl Kraeling to Dean of the Faculties R. Wendell Harrison, December 14, 1956.

[56] "Das megalomane Dictionary-project wird mit der grössten Unlust von Oppenheim betrieben, Gelb gibt theoretische Richtlinien heraus und hofft, dass er notleidende Emigranten finden wird, die daran arbeiten; ich fungiere als hineinredender Kiebitz." (Landsberger to Kraus, December 9, 1953.)

[57] "Zunächst ist Gelbs SOP als zu kompliziert, zu starr und nicht zweckdienlich *abzulehnen.* "

[58] Landsberger, *Remarks on SOP* (memorandum of spring 1954) p. 7.

[59] ibid. page 2.

[60] Oppenheim, *Contributions to the Discussions of SOP* (memorandum of spring 1954).

[61] ibid.

[62] Richard T. Hallock, memorandum to the CAD staff, February 9, 1955.

[63] For an illustration of the first drafts of the very first words written for the Assyrian Dictionary, see Appendix 2.

[64] A. L. Oppenheim, *Letters from Mesopotamia*, part II. Chicago: University of Chicago Press, 1967.

[65] "… ich in diese Hetze hineingeraten bin, für die Reiner ein Akrobatentalent ohne Gleichen entwickelt hat (blitzschnell, aber nicht schlampig oder halb!). Ich mache mich weiter als Fehlerdetektor und als Lexicograph (im alten Sinne) tätig." (Landsberger to Kraus, December 11, 1956).

[66] "Ich habe nun 4 Monate damit zugebracht, alle Artikel mit ḫₓy neu zu schreiben. Ich musste es tun, weil sie so schlecht waren." (March 18, 1955.)

[67] The annual (now biennial) summer institute of the Linguistic Society of America was held in Chicago in 1954.

[68] Eventually published as "Lexicography, Lexicology, and the Akkadian Dictionary," in *Estructuralismo e historia: miscelánea homenaje a André Martinet*, vol. II, pp. 63–75 (see note 46).

[69] "The letter to Falkenstein has been written (in German by Karl himself) upon a meeting of the board and von Soden is now released. At that very meeting Karl ("Der Knabe Karl beginnt mir unheimlich zu werden") dropped a bombshell by suggesting that instead of preparing a 'torso' of a dictionary at great expense we should think of assisting von Soden in his work by supplying him with the material we have accumulated. He spoke of the obvious 'dictionary-fatigue' of some members of the board and the rising costs caused by the inevitable promotions of Rowton and Reiner and Hallock in the course of the years ahead, not to speak of the difficulties [here the bottom line of the page is missing]…

Assyriology would be better served if we would all collaborate to bring out the vocabularies in the shortest possible period rather than to help von Soden if—if— we have to abandon the project."

[70] Oppenheim to Landsberger, October 10, 1954.

[71] Landsberger to Kraeling, September 5, 1954.

[72] "Die 'Constitution' von 1952, die durch meine Revolte zustande kam, und über die Jay heute noch nicht wegkommt, die er (anscheinend zum Schluss erfolglos) sabotiert, betrachte ich nach wie vor für richtig und segensreich. … Sie haben die Schlüsselstellung und ich kann nichts tun als Sie dabei stützen und unterstützen. Erstens soll das Recht, über das Dict. zu bestimmen denen einzuräumen, die bisher am meisten dafür geleistet haben. Ohne meinen Beitrag zu unterschätzen, ist kein Zweifel, dass Sie den weitaus grössten Anteil haben. Der Anteil der übrigen Mitglieder des board ist in realistischer Weise abzuschätzen. Ihre natürliche Bescheidenheit muss ihnen sagen, wieweit sie das Recht haben mitzureden. Ein 'Aufsichtsrat' kann gewiss nur nützen, und es muss Karl unbenommen bleiben, objektive Urteile wie etwa das Güterbocks, Goetze's, Speisers einzuholen.

'Allright', wird einer sagen, der mir bisher willig gefolgt ist. 'Ist aber Quantität alles? Liegt bei unserem Leo nicht die Gefahr vor, dass er sich in eine hektische Eile hineintreiben lässt, Fertigbringen um jeden Preis? Insbesondre wenn ihm noch ein höheres Ziel, etwa eine Kulturgeschichte, vorschwebt?' Darauf habe ich zu erwidern:

1) Ohne ein gewisses Stabbrechen und Durchschlagen gordischer Knoten geht es bei keinem von uns ab, ganz besonders charakteristisch ist diese Eigenschaft für unseren Konkurrenten v. S.;

2) Leo weisst, dass es sich um ein wissenschaftliches Projekt handelt und dass der Sinn eines solchen ist, *in Ruhe* an den Problemen zu arbeiten;

3) Solange Landsberger aktiv ist, gibt er eine gewisse Gewähr, auch sonst ist es Leos Art, die Fragen mit den Kollegen durchzusprechen;

4) Wenn dieser Punkt entscheidend ist, muss eben das Projekt aufgegeben werden.

Taktik

a) Leo muss nach reiflicher Überlegung die Entscheidung treffen, ob er das Dict. als seine Lebensaufgabe übernehmen will. Vermutlich wird ihm noch ein stattlicher Lebensrest für andere Aufgaben übrig bleiben;

b) Karl muss überzeugt werden; es genügt nicht, ihm ein lahmes Ja oder stillschweigenden Konsens abzuringen. Er, und seine ev. Berater (die ich leicht beeinflussen kann; deren—mit mir übereinstimmende—Meinung ich z. T. schon eingeholt habe) werden nur überzeugt werden können, wenn ein *Wörterbuch* gemacht und nicht Buchstaben gekotzt werden; wenn ihm (ihnen) plausibel gemacht wird dass von Sodens Werk nicht dupliziert wird.

c) Im Board muss die 3:1 Majorität rücksichtslos ausgespielt werden. Zunächst ist Gelbs SOP als zu kompliziert, zu starr und nicht zweckdienlich *abzulehnen*, sodann das Landsberger-Oppenheim SOP, *das ich bis zu meiner Rückkunft zu for-mulieren bitte*, (kurz, aber nicht zu vage, unter Berücksichtigung von unten S. 8) *anzunehmen*, dann die general procedure der künftigen Arbeit, gleichfalls im Wege der Stimmenmehrheit, zu beschliessen.

Bitte gehen Sie keine krummen Wege, keine Überrumplung Jay's, keine "Taktiken"; kein Zustand, wo ein Ochse des team dorthin, der andere dorthin zieht! Nur durch all diese Unklarheit, Feigheit, double talk ist die Atmosphäre des 3. Stocks vergiftet worden. Sicher war Jay stets eine bequeme Ausrede für unsre eigene inefficiency, Uninteressiertheit, bzw. die Vermeidung des Eingeständnisses, das das ganze Projekt unreif und megalomanisch ist. Andrerseits sind wir drei und sämtliche andren Assyriologen uns darüber einig, dass Jay nicht der Mann ist, an der Spitze eines teams zu stehen, das ein akk. Wb. macht. Schon jetzt, nach relativ so kurzer Zeit hat er gezeigt, dass er es nur zu Tode organisieren kann. Weder kann er Fachleute unseres Kalibers "bossen" noch die jüngeren Mitarbeiter, die nicht "gebosst", sondern von erfahrenen Experten angeleitet werden sollen. Wenn Th. und Sie glauben, dass eine Kaltstellung Jay's aus Gründen der Freundschaft und anderen persönlichen Motiven untunlich sei, dann möchte ich empfehlen, das project radikal aufzugeben, und auch eventuelle Ersatz-Projekte so zu gestalten, dass Jay's Aufgabenkreis von dem unsrigen *klar abgegrenzt* ist. Aber vielleicht ist dieser Gesichtspunkt nicht massgebend, denn Karl ist für solche "kalte Kuren" der ide-ale Doktor, und vielleicht dämmert es jetzt in Jay selbst, dass seine wahre Stärke und Zukunft nicht auf dem Gebiete der "Semasiologie" liegt." (Landsberger to Oppenheim, late October 1954.)

[73] Here he refers to his office in the Oriental Institute, which, in fact, was not Room 309, but Room 316.

[74] Letter of October 19, 1954.

[75] "Wie ich schon an Erika geschrieben habe, ist mir 309 Orinst der schönste Aufenthaltsort und der third floor—trotz allem—das liebste Milieu. Ich freue mich in Ihrem Briefe zu lesen, dass diese Sympathien nicht ganz einseitig sind."

[76] Kraeling to Board of Editors, December 3, 1954.

[77] Board of Editors to Kraeling, December 1, 1954.

[78] Kraeling to Alexander Heidel, December 22, 1954.

[79] For example, he suggested that lines on the page be numbered so that they could be referred to easily; he also objected to insufficiently abbreviated references, which in his opinion would add to the price of the volumes.

[80] For the minutes of one such meeting see Appendix 4.

[81] "liebevolle Versenkung."

[82] "Oppenheim hat vor etwa 1 Woche offiziell taken over; er ist für 3 Jahre editor in charge, aber nur, wie die drei andren für 1 Jahr editor (versteht sich vom 1. Juli 55 bis 30 Juni 56). ... Demnach werde ich ab 1. Juli (Emeritierungsdatum) inshal-lah nur noch als editor mein (bisheriges) Gehalt beziehen ... Meine Aufgabe ist es, die von Oppi, Reiner, Rowton gelieferten Entwürfe durchzusehen und druckfer-tig zu machen. Sie wird dadurch verbessert, aber auch erschwert, dass Jacobsen in sie eingebaut ist, und ich gleichzeitig das von ihm gelieferte Sumerisch einerseits,

wie überhaupt alles mit ihm diskutiere. Die grosse Frage ist, ob wir schnell genug sind, den von Oppi versprochenen speed zu halten." (Landsberger to Kraus, December 8, 1954.)

[83] "I spend a part of every day in discussing with Benno [Landsberger] the difficult passages and lexical problems that come up in the course of his day's work. A special responsibility devolving on me in these discussions is to adduce relevant passages from the large unilingual Sumerian materials, passages which are frequently crucial to the correct understanding of an Accadian word." (Jacobsen to Oppenheim, October 26, 1958.)

[84] Landsberger, *Remarks on SOP* (memorandum of spring 1954) p. 1.

[85] Latin translation of *plein anagkê, zên ouk anagkê* Plutarch, Pomp. 50.

[86] The original estimate was 958 pages, revised to 1,500 pages, with the final manuscript projected to be completed in 1985 and published in 1986.

[87] Breasted, *The Oriental Institute* (1933), p. 400, cited in Stolper, *News and Notes* 129 (May–June 1991), p. 2b end.

[88] Gelb to Jacobsen, director of the Oriental Institute, October 18, 1949.

[89] Stolper, pp. 2 and 10.

[90] E-mail from Randall Garr, February 17, 1998.

[91] See *Wie die Blätter am Baum, so wechseln die Wörter. 100 Jahre Thesaurus Linguae Latinae*. Vorträge der Veranstaltungen am 29. und 30. Juni 1994 in München, ed. Dietrich Krömer. Stuttgart & Leipzig: Teubner, 1995.

[92] To render an Akkadian phrase into idiomatic English often tends to obfuscate the intention of the original.

[93] Bowman to Oppenheim, March 2, 1962.

[94] Bowman to Reiner, April 30, 1962.

[95] George G. Cameron, professor at the University of Michigan, and a former collaborator on the CAD, wrote a scathing letter to Oppenheim about this procedure.

[96] Kraeling to Oppenheim, December 17, 1958.

[97] *The Elamite Language* (= Altkleinasiatische Sprachen, Part II), B. Spuler, ed., Handbuch der Orientalistik, Erste Abteilung, Band II, Lieferung 2. Leiden: E. J. Brill, 1969; *A Linguistic Analysis of Akkadian*. The Hague: Mouton, 1966.

[98] *The Linguistic Reporter*, 11:6 (December 1969) 94–97.

[99] *Orientalia* NS 21 (1952) 359.

[100] "…the sum total [of the number of lines] would leave the Rigveda (about the size of the Iliad) and the Homeric epics, as well as the Old and New Testaments…far behind" A. L. Oppenheim, *Ancient Mesopotamia*. Chicago: University of Chicago Press, 1964, pp. 17f.

[101] T. Jacobsen, *The Treasures of Darkness*. New Haven and London: Yale University Press, 1976.

[102] "Dass Jacobsen die Grenze zwischen Genie und.… [sic! dots in text] schon überschritten hat, muss jedem klar werden, der seine sowohl für Sum. wie Akk. gültigen -i, -u, -a Schemen ansieht." (Landsberger to Kraus, February 5, 1961.)

[103] W. von Soden, *Grundriss der akkadischen Grammatik* (see note 33).

[104] J. A. Brinkman, *Bibliotheca Orientalis* 23 (1965) 295f.

[105] There are no transcripts of the Editorial Board's meetings, but we have an exchange of letters between Jacobsen and Oppenheim following one such meeting.

[106] Kraeling to Oppenheim, November 6, 1958.

[107] Oppenheim memo to Kraeling, March 4, 1959.

[108] The date of the end of Kraeling's term as director of the Oriental Institute.

[109] Oppenheim memo to Kraeling, March 4, 1959.

[110] Kraeling to Jacobsen, April 1, 1959.

[111] Kraeling memorandum to the voting members of the Oriental Institute, April 1, 1959.

[112] Jacobsen to the CAD staff, April 15, 1959, see Appendix 5. The repeated reference to power (the "power" of the editor-in-charge and the "power of decision") in this letter reveals one of the deeper reasons of Jacobsen's attitude toward the Dictionary as run by Oppenheim: Jacobsen obviously resented that he did not wield power equal or superior to Oppenheim's although he considered that Oppenheim had reached his status through his own, Jacobsen's, efforts and mediation.

[113] Jacobsen to voting members on November 17, 1959 (meeting chaired by Wilson; Kraeling refused to attend).

[114] Memorandum of 20 pages. Some of the allegations, often too unrealistic or even absurd to merit rebuttal, such as "Articles were being withheld from the editors if Dr. Oppenheim thought the editor might deal with them too carefully. Dr. Gelb had expressed a wish to return to the work and Dr. Oppenheim kept him out. If he [Landsberger] should wish to write a journal article he may do so if he can get permission from Dr. Oppenheim, otherwise not" were nonetheless refuted in Oppenheim's response. Landsberger's own judgment of the editor's attitude toward his contributions was stated in his *Opinion* on the Assyrian Dictionary: "A personal remark: I am deeply indebted to the CAD because it has been the vehicle enabling thousands of details and also essential viewpoints of mine to reach the public, points which otherwise would have been relegated to oblivion. The fairness of the acting editors in handling this material must be stressed."

[115] Landsberger himself acknowledged this in a December 24, 1959, letter to Kraus: "Jacobsen ist der Irrenanstalt näher als Oppenheim, der *nur* 'schwer nervös' ist."

[116] The statement in its entirety appears as Appendix 6.

[117] Later published as "Hebrew Lexicography: Informal Thoughts," in *Linguistics and Biblical Hebrew*, Walter Bodine, ed. Winona Lake, Indiana: Eisenbrauns, 1992, pp. 137–151.

[118] Loc. cit. p. 146. Another statement of Barr's that deserves the attention of the Akkadian lexicographer is, "The dictionary is not a mere registration of the signs found on paper in the traditional text; it is a registration of the lexical elements that functioned in the language," p. 150.

[119] This was the volume in the works when Jacobsen resigned from the Editorial Board and the manuscript of which, partially annotated by Jacobsen, was destroyed at his request by the director.

[120] Landsberger's friend F. R. Kraus also lobbied for the preservation of the CAD. In a letter dated January 24, 1961, he says, "I am really feeling miserable, almost sick, wenn ich von den Streitereien um das CAD höre. Die Veröffentlichung des CAD aufzugeben, wäre ein Verbrechen gegen die Assyriologie und bedeutete den Selbstmord des Or. Inst. Ohne CAD sollte man das Or. Inst. sofort auflösen und als Institut zur Erforschung des social behaviour der Mikroben auf dem Mars und der Venus neu einrichten. Das CAD ist ein absolutes Bedürfnis der Assyriologie und wir sind tief dankbar dafür, dass wir es so, wie es ist, haben.... Ich persönlich kann nur ergebenst-dringlich bitten, das CAD weiterzupublizieren, und feurig hoffen, dass dieses an sich schon unglaublich schwierige Unternehmen nicht durch überflüssige, kraftzehrende Reibereien noch erschwert wird."

[121] Landsberger to Jacobsen, February 7, 1961.

[122] "Ein Kompromiss ist unwahrscheinlich, Gelb und ich versuchen." (Landsberger to Kraus, February 5, 1961).

[123] Kraeling to Reiner, September 3, 1960.

[124] Statement to the staff of the CAD, copy to Acting Chancellor R. W. Harrison, January 31, 1961.

[125] Jacobsen letters to the voting members of the Oriental Institute, April 4, 1962.

[126] Adams to Levi, May 21, 1962.

[127] Evidently, Landsberger could envisage them only as competing!

[128] "Frivolously" stands for intended "recklessly."

[129] Apud Oppenheim, *Orientalia* NS 37 (1968) 367–370.

[130] I. J. Gelb, *A Study of Writing*. Chicago: University of Chicago Press, 1952.

[131] I. J. Gelb, *Computer-aided Analysis of Amorite* (Assyriological Studies, 21). Chicago: Oriental Institute, 1980.

[132] See the obituary by J. A. Brinkman, *Archiv für Orientforschung* 34 (1987) 252–253.

[133] For the names of collaborators from 1963 to 1996 see Appendix 1.

[134] Kraeling to Reiner, September 3, 1960, cited above, p. 60.

[135] On page vi of his *Opinion* on the Assyrian Dictionary.

[136] M. W. Stolper, *News and Notes* 129 (May–June 1991) 10.

[137] Oppenheim, "In memoriam Benno Landsberger," *Orientalia* NS 37 (1968) 367–370.

[138] For the contributions of Geers see the appraisal by Oppenheim, *Journal of Near Eastern Studies* 33 (1954) 179f., in one of the two issues dedicated to Geers's memory.

[139] Reiner to J. A. Brinkman, November 1974.

[140] For example, AHw.'s wabālu(m) was published as abālu A; uṣû(m) I under muṣû.

[141] In fact, I was told in 1985 that the changeover to computers cost the *Middle English Dictionary* the loss of one year of work.

[142] Jack M. Sasson: English-Akkadian Analytical Index to the Chicago Assyrian Dictionary. Part I. Chapel Hill, NC: n.p., 1973.

LIST OF COLLABORATORS FROM 1963 TO 1996

This list continues the list prepared by I. J. Gelb and published in the Introduction to Volume A Part 1, 1963.

Astakhishvili, Erekle	1990–1991
Biggs, Robert D.	1963–
Black, Jeremy A.	1980–1982
Brinkman, John A.	1963–64 part time; 1964–65; 1965–67 part time
Caplice, Richard J.	1971–72 part time; 1974–75 part time; 1978–79; 1985 (6 months)
Edzard, Dietz O.	1981 (2 months); 1984 (5 months); 1985 and 1989 (2 months each)
Gallery, Maureen	1976–79
Groneberg, Brigitte	1976–77; 1987 (2 1/2 months)
Hirsch, Hans E.	1960–61; 1978–79 (editing R), continued editing for a time in Vienna
Hunger, Hermann	1970–73; 1976–78; returned for three- to four-month periods in 1981, 1983, 1985, 1987, 1989, 1991, 1993, 1995; wrote Š and R articles in Vienna in 1978–79
Jas, Remigius	1992–93; 1994–95
Kienast, Burkhart	1958–60; 1967–69 part time; 1973–74 part time; returned for two- to five-month periods in 1982, 1983, 1985, 1987, 1990, and 1991
Ludwig, Marie-Christine	1988–89
Mattila, Raija	1996
Oelsner, Joachim	1983 (6 months)
Parpola, Simo	1982 (6 months); 1985 (3 months); 1989 (2 months)
Renger, Johannes M.	1966–76; returned for two- or three-month periods in 1980, 1982, 1985, 1988, 1989, 1990
Riemschneider, Kaspar	1974–75
Rochberg, Francesca	1977–78; 1979–80; 1980–83 (one-third time)
Roth, Martha T.	1979–
van Soldt, Wilfred H.	1989
Stol, Marten	1973–74
Stolper, Matthew W.	1978–79 (6 months), 1980–
Sweet, Ronald F. G.	1956–57; 1958–59 part time; 1967–68 part time

Veenhof, Klaas	1979 (6 months)
Weisberg, David	1965–67
Westenholz, Joan G.	1978–79; 1982–84
Wiggermann, Frans	1986 (9 months)

This list does not include the research associates for the Materials for the Sumerian Lexicon Project (MSL) under Benno Landsberger and Miguel Civil.

EARLY DRAFTS FOR THE H VOLUME

Oppenheim preserved a few early drafts "for historical interest only," in a notebook, dated April 2, 1956, which he prefaced as follows:

> This Notebook contains the first drafts of the first words ever written up for the Assyrian Dictionary. All other drafts and manuscripts for the first volume of the Dictionary (Vol. VI) were destroyed upon publication of the first volume in April 1956.

The preserved drafts were written by Reiner or Rowton in 1953 and 1954, edited, with changes made in the translations, by Oppenheim and finally by Gelb; they are dated to month and year, and were initialled EO (Elizabeth Oppenheim) after having been proofread by Mrs. Oppenheim.

I. ḪZN ḫazānūtu, ḫazannūtu, ḫaziannuttu "office of the ~mayor~ ((ḫazannu)"

II. ~Subst., f.~

III. ~Attested in~ MA, Nuzi, NA

X. ana ḫa-zi-a-nu-ut-te il-[....] (KAV 217:4 MA ~soon.~)
šakin māti ᴸᵁrēsišu ana ᴸᵁḫa-za-nu-ti usēseb/after the
death of the king (ABL 473:6, NA ~la.~) *the governor of the country installed his*
the officers (lit: aide-de-comp.) in
[before?] they appointed PN a-na ḫa-za-nu-tu, sartennu *the office of the mayor*
exercised judgment (ABL 716 rev. 14, NA ~la.~)

Nuzi in dates: šuntu Kuššḫ-ḫarbe ina Nuzi ḫa-za-an-nu-ta *at that time K was*
îpuš (JEN 46:24; 252:46; etc.), ~variant of the date-~ *in office as mayor of*
~formula discussed under ḫazannu.~ *Nuzi*

Dec. 1953

Reiner
Oppenheim
Gelb

I HTT   (hattu) in   bēl ḫatti: ## s.; ##   "lord of the scepter"
                                                    " death with the scepter"
II   → scepter bearer; ## SB; ##

III chapter in his H

IV cf. the right hattu, etc.

V lizziz Papsukkal bēl GIŠ.PA lirīq mursu##may P., lord of the staff, stand
by [that] sickness may be removed## (Šurpu IV 97). H.

XII hattu is the symbol of the messenger (sukkallu), cf. sub hattu V a.

Mar. 1954

Reiner
Oppenheim
JCb

I HZR   (huzīru) ## s. ## "hog"; ##   "pig"

II Subst. m.
      from O Akk. on; ##
III OA and in PN
              c
IV Cf. huzirtu.   ?

IX hu-zi-ru = ša-hu-u ## LTBA 2 13:13 and dupl.

P(a) in gen. ## ## šu-ma hu-zi-ru lá i-ka-b[e-ru...] ## if the pigs do not get fat ##
              6   OA Let.; ###
        (BIN VI 84:35, Capp.)
              KAL   ## x minas of   14   OA Let.
      x MA.NA Ì.   ša hu-zi-ri-im pork lard ## (TCL XIV 47:5, Capp.)

P(b) as   PN: (, p. 199 Ur III; RA IX 57 Nr. 12 r., 1 Ur III,
                             10, 65:20, 123:19, 212:20 OAkk.)
        (2) Hu-zi-ra (HSS p.   Nuzi)
        Hu-zi-ri (both m. and f.) ref. in OIP LVII , 66, Nuzi)
        (3) Hu-zi-ri (Strassm. Cyr. 287:40; ABL 1442 rev. 1,   )

hu-zi-ra ## HSS 10 65:20, OAkk, ## also ibid. 123:19 and 212:20; ### hu-zi-ri ## AOS 32
188, Ur II, ## also RA 9 57 No. 12 r. 1; ### hu-zi-ri ## ABL 1442 r. 1, NA, ## also Cyr.
287:40; ### cf. ## hu-zi-ri ## [masc. and fem., derivation uncert.] ## OIP 57 66, Nuzi.
P XIII Landsberger, Fauna, 101.

Jan. 1954,

Reiner
Oppenheim
Selb

EO

EXCERPT FROM A LETTER OF KRAELING, JUNE 28, 1955, ABOUT AUGUSTIN

Excerpt From Dr. Kraeling's Letter

New Haven
June 28, 1955

"Had a long session this morning with Mr. Augustine on which I would like to report. Will you be good enough to have Leo see what I report herewith. I covered most of the things we shall need to know about in taking the next steps. I inquired about his current commitments, his sources of paper, his means of communication, his set-up here and abroad, the probabilities as he sees them of an upswing in Germany in the standard of living and consequent rise in prices for compostion and materials in the course of the foreseeable future and obtained in general a favorable picture. In Augustine's judgment the thing to do would be to have the Oriental Institute publish and to have distribution undertaken in Europe and overseas by Augustine, Hamburg and in the U.S.A. by either ourselves or the UofC Press. To bring this about we give orders for printing, volume by volume and sign a contract only concerning publication. If we pay for the printing outright in accordance with estimates made on each volume, the contract for overseas distribution would bring us in 75 percent of the net income from sales, the other 25 to be kept by Augustine and to cover the cost of sales promotion, billing, shipping to buyers, storing, postage, wrapping etc. Net is the sum total of receipts from sales, though not sales in every instance at list price, but sales at such discounts as it may be necessary to give to book-sellers and agents. (This is better than I had expected, for, as I said to Leo, I was ready to settle for 50 percent of net). We would have to a) obtain from Roger Shugg written permission to publish

ourselves; b) an agreement to distribute to American customers at
some figure like the 25 percent from net that Augustine will get for
distribution overseas; c) do our own distribution instead, if we
prefer; d) make sure that distribution by U.ofC. Press does not involve a conflict of priority rights between Augustine and book dealers
overseas with which the U.ofC. Press may have special agreements for ex-
clusive handling of its listed items. Augustine has agreed to send to
Leo at Chicago a draft of a publication and distribution agreement for
inspection at our August 1 meeting. Augustine feels that an edition of
750 copies plus might be better than 1,000, that the projected price
of $10 (40 marks) is good and not prohibitive aborad. He says the costs
as given in the estimate are f.o.b. Chicago and that all import duties
are covered by them. He agrees to report annually on net income balances,
overseas income to be applied to the publication of succeeding volumes, as
previously suggested. If Leo and the boys can keep from rewriting the
volume in proof and can deep up with the European production tempo, he
believes that text submitted not later than Nov. 1 will assure delivery
by February March and permit setting April 1 as the official publication
date.

"We spent much time discussiong sales procedure, more particularly
orders versus subscription, and both he and I were of a divided mind as
to which was preferable. This much is clear that he should have in hand
soon copy for a four-page folder that will announce the publication. The
first page would give the title of the work and the editors and the arrangements about publication and distribution (as outlined above). The
second page would have a general statement about the background and
purpose of the publication, to be prepared by Leo. The third would give
a sample page of the text (as already prepared). The fourth would give
some idea of the organization of the entire work as Leo and the boys vis-
ualize it. The material for such a folder A. would like to have (must
have, he said) before August 14, when he will be going overseas again
for a while. This will be set up and lists will be prepared during the
fall for distribution, so that when Leo sends the manuscript over on
Nov. 1 the folders can be mailed at that time. With the folder there
would be sent out either a simple order card or an order card and a
subscription card. In case we allow people to subscribe it would be

necessary to say that those who subscribe by March 1 would get their copies 15 days in advance of publication and at a discount of ten percent
of list. I forgot to say that page four of the folder should indicate
not only the plan for the distribution of the material in volumes, but
should also indicate that there is a general relationship between price
and size of the several volumes, e.g. that Vol. H between 250 and 300 pages
would sell for $10.00 and Vol. G (between --- pages and --- pages) for
$ ---/ . Subscription arrangements are not absolutely necessary since
one can receive orders for "continuations" as well as for individual
volumes. During the early fall we would work out with him lists of
addresses for recipients of the folder in this country and abroad and
he would co-ordinate our lists and his own existing lists of buyers of
Orientalia abroad and do the mailing himself from Locust Valley. Also
he pays all the costs of printing and mailing the announcements and
puts out a German as well as an English edition of the folder."

MINUTES (EXCERPTS) OF NOVEMBER 19, 1958, BOARD MEETING

ASSYRIAN DICTIONARY PROJECT,
MINUTES OF THE BOARD MEETING,
HELD IN THE DIRECTOR'S OFFICE
OF THE ORIENTAL INSTITUTE OF
THE UNIVERSITY OF CHICAGO, ON
NOVEMBER 19, 1958.

Present were: Ignace J. Gelb
Thorkild Jacobsen
Benno Landsberger
A. Leo Oppenheim

The meeting was called by Mr. Oppenheim, as ex-officio chairman of the Board, upon the request contained in a letter of the Director of the Oriental Institute, Dr. Carl H. Kraeling, and it began at 4:00 P.M.

Mr. Oppenheim proposed that the meeting should be organized in three stages:

1) A report on the present state of the work on the Assyrian Dictionary,

2) A discussion of Dr. Kraeling's suggestions concerning the Editor-in-Charge,

3) A discussion of proposals to be made by Dr. Jacobsen.

Dr. Oppenheim proposed to chair only Parts I and III of the meeting; Dr. Landsberger was to chair Part II. This was accepted by the members of the Board.

Part I.

Mr. Oppenheim informed the Board members of two new appointments, that of Dr. Kienast and of Mr. Sweet.

Mr. Oppenheim discussed at length the progress of the volumes of the Assyrian Dictionary. Some of the points he made are:

Volume I is slowly progressing because Father Moran had finished only one third of this volume and Miss Reiner and Mr. Oppenheim are doing the remaining two thirds; Dr. Landsberger has about four fifths of it on his desk, of which he has done about half. This volume will be presented to the Board in the spring when there will be another meeting.

The completion of future volumes will be done in this order: first the three
S volumes, and then either Volume B or Volume A. The draft of the S volumes should be
finished in the fall of 1959 and then work on Volume A could be started.

The Volume A could not be started this year according to plan due to the un-
certainty in the number of collaborators who would be available to work on the project.
The basic problems of organization are solved now, and it appears that the three
volumes (S, Ş and Z) could be done at the same time. But this likewise depends upon
the state of the personnel problem. Mr. Sweet, e.g., will be teaching at Potomac
University for a summer term and will probably be gone in a year or two. There is,
of course, Dr. Rowton, and, as Dr. Kienast is working out well, if he were here another
year, Volume A would have a better chance of being started. Volume A may take two or
three years to complete.

Mr. Oppenheim then proposed that the committee vote on whether Dr. Kienast be
recommended to continue with the Assyrian Dictionary Project for another year as no
one else was considered for next year as yet. It was mentioned that a decision about
Dr. Kienast need be reached by December because his passage back to Germany had to be
secured·by the Fulbright Committee. After much discussion on Dr. Kienast's qualities,
the advantages and disadvantages of keeping him here as opposed to using new students
on the project, and after making it clear that Dr. Kienast was well aware of the fact
that this position would not be permanent but would be for just one year, it was agreed
and voted by all present that Dr. Kienast be recommended to Dr. Kraeling for continuation for an additional year.

PART II (chaired by Dr. Landsberger)

Mr. Landsberger opened this section by stating that the discussion was concerned
with the continuing of Dr. Oppenheim as Editor-in-Charge of the Assyrian Dictionary
Project.

Mr. Jacobsen pointed out that the Board needed first to vote on the Editor-in-
Charge for specific volumes and that a vote to confirm authority for each individual
volume was essential. He said the Board should continue in its basic set up and that
the Board should decide by a series of votes to confirm Dr. Oppenheim's authority for
each volume already published.

Mr. Landsberger then moved that the Board vote to give Mr. Oppenheim the authority for volumes G, E, and D. It was observed that Volume G had already been voted on and approved at a previous meeting. Mr. Jacobsen said the Board also needed an affirmative vote assigning the authority to publish Volume G to Mr. Oppenheim. All voted on Volumes E, D, and G, and Mr. Oppenheim was given authority on each of these volumes.

Mr. Landsberger then asked if anyone wanted to propose any changes in the present positions of Miss Reiner and Mr. Oppenheim within the Assyrian Dictionary Project, or if these positions should be left without interference.

Mr. Jacobsen proposed to let the running of the Dictionary remain as is. He commented on the excellent job that was being done, remarked that no work of this kind could be perfect, but must be looked at as a whole and is something that everyone can be proud of. He was in favor of affirming Mr. Oppenheim as Editor-in-Charge, and he thought Mr. Oppenheim should be given the same authority for Volume I as he had been given for E, G, D, and H.

Mr. Gelb suggested voting Mr. Oppenheim the authority for Volumes I and B together, but Mr. Jacobsen said the Board should at this time just consider Volume I. Mr. Landsberger confirmed Mr. Jacobsen's suggestion. Unanimously Mr. Oppenheim was given the authority for Volume I.

Mr. Landsberger mentioned that he supposed Erica Reiner's work on the Dictionary was implied. Mr. Jacobsen said that this was not the case; the Board was voting only for the authority given the Editor-in-Charge.

Mr. Gelb expressed surprise that work on Volume B was going wrong and he asked why the work had been discontinued. Mr. Oppenheim replied that Mr. Rowton, who had wanted a volume of his own to work on, had been given B. After nineteen months he delivered a manuscript of about half, the other half not having been touched. At present about one third of Volume B is finished and it would take him and Miss Reiner perhaps half a year to complete it. Now, as everyone on the project needs help, which takes up a good deal of Mr. Oppenheim's and Miss Reiner's time, Mr. Oppenheim thought it best to let Volume B rest awhile.

Then Dr. Oppenheim told about the new procedure for drafting the articles which is now being used, and which entails intensive collaboration with each person working on the project, and discussions of individual problems.

Mr. Jacobsen expressed surprise that Volume B was as large as Volume E. He mentioned the time that would be involved in working on this large a volume and said the assurance of the same staff or of a necessary staff must be had. It was therefore best to vote on working on a smaller volume because of the now-available staff. Dr. Oppenheim mentioned that there were very few small letters left. Dr. Landsberger said there needs be no formal decision as yet on Volume B. In reply, Mr. Jacobsen said there is a great need for formal decision, and he suggested Mr. Oppenheim be given authority on Volume B through a formal vote. However, no vote was taken.

Mr. Oppenheim and Mr. Jacobsen brought up the subject of the S volumes. It was moved that a vote be taken on giving Mr. Oppenheim authority for the volumes S, Ṣ and Z. The vote was taken and unanimously approved. It was also voted and approved that Mr. Oppenheim was to edit the S volumes after Volume I.

Then Mr. Oppenheim made the point that Miss Reiner is already Associate editor. He said this was decided at an earlier meeting, at which Miss Reiner was appointed Associate editor with no salary. Mr. Jacobsen suggested a formal vote of approval that Erica Reiner is Associate editor. All voted unanimous approval.

Part II of the meeting ended and Mr. Oppenheim thanked Mr. Landsberger for acting as chairman during that section.

JACOBSEN'S MEMO OF APRIL 15, 1959

THE UNIVERSITY OF CHICAGO

DATE 15 April 1959

To Members of the Assyrian Dictionary Staff DEPARTMENT Oriental Institute

FROM Thorkild Jacobsen   DEPARTMENT Oriental Institute

IN RE:

It is proper that you should know that I handed in my resignation as Editor on the Dictionary Project on March 13 of this year and that, at my insistence, it was finally accepted on April 1.

The reasons which compelled me to take this step are that recent events have tended to concentrate all effective power in the hand of the Editor-in-Charge and have rendered the system of checks and balances hitherto prevailing inoperative. It has always been my position that the announced policy of the Dictionary (vol. 6 p. vii) must be interpreted so as to permit a reasonable degree of penetration and in a few special cases even maximal penetration. It is likewise my firm conviction that actual power of decision in Dictionary matters should lie with the board as a whole rather than with any single person.

Since I see no effective means of maintaining these to me essential features of the work it has seemed correct to me not to continue in a position of responsibility which could be of responsibility in name only.

I cannot believe that discussion could do much of a positive nature to clarify further the principles stated above. Lapse from the level of principle in private or public discussion will obviously do only harm and may severely damage the reputation of the Oriental Institute.

Thorkild Jacobsen

To: Mr. Gelb
    Mr. Landsberger
    ✓Mr. Oppenheim
    Mr. Rowton
    Miss Reiner
    Mr. Sweet
    Mr. Kienast

STATEMENT OF OPPENHEIM, DECEMBER 1959

I shall not take much of your time because I consider other scholars' time at least as valuable as my own, and because I do not enjoy preaching to a captive audience.

You listened a few weeks ago to a lengthy personal attack launched against myself (and, to a lesser degree, Dr. Kraeling) by Dr. Jacobsen, ending with one of his characteristic turn-abouts, a proposal for a vote of confidence in the Director, with some addenda about whose interpretation there may be a considerable difference of opinion. I shall not defend the Director; he is well able to defend himself. Nor shall I bother you unduly with the quibblings of Assyriologists. I shall inform you in as brief a space as possible of the real nature of the alleged errors on my part so rhetorically described by Dr. Jacobsen, seeking only to correct his most obvious distortions of the truth. I also intend to tell you why I cannot work any longer with a man of his type.

Dr. Jacobsen listed, all told, 12 so-called mistakes. Of these, two were actual mistakes; two were typographical errors, as can be shown from the original MS; two are omissions of a word in a translation; two were errors in references left there by himself when he corrected the phrasing of the typescript; two concern moot points where one can legitimately differ, and two are no mistakes at all in the CAD, but are his. Details are listed on an attached sheet.

What boils down in the end is that Dr. Jacobsen, in spite of his evident ill will, could find 8 mistakes in the approximately 1200 quotations that make up the article epesu. Actually there are more mistakes - as we know from our files of corrections, of the existence of which Dr. Jacobsen has no idea because he has not been sufficiently interested in the actual work going on. I could easily draw up a list of similar mistakes that have escaped Dr. Jacobsen's attention when he was working as editor,

or of mistakes he entered into the MS which had to be taken out again after consultation with the other editors.   However, such a procedure I consider beneath my
dignity and the dignity of this Institute.

Let me correct now a number of conscious distortions offered by Dr. Jacobsen,
distortions which I can only regard as consciously put forward. I shall be quite
brief:

It is not true that the MS of vol. H. was sent to the printer without obtaining
the board's release;

It is not true that articles were withheld from editors;

It is not true that I replied to Dr. Jacobsen's suggestion for calling a
meeting with a refusal to comply with the statute;

It is not true that I ever refused any request of Dr. Gelb's to work on the
Project; I have always gratefully accepted his contributions.

It is not true that the members of the editorial board were forbidden by me
to publish their opposition to certain interpretations of a given word; a vote was
taken on this issue and all the other editors voted against Dr. Jacobsen. He
apparently does not play the democracy game when it turn against him.

It is not true that Dr. Landsberger ever did, much less ever had, to ask my
permission to write a journal article. In fact, the length of his bibliography
during the last five years is rather impressive. The other accusations with regard
to Dr. Landsberger are ~~even more~~ too absurd ~~and can only be ignored~~ to be mentioned.

And as to the title page, it is common knowledge that it was designed by
Dr. Jacobsen together with Margaret Bell Cameron; this is the first time I have
heard that Dr. Jacobsen does not like it any more. I am open to propositions to
change it.

As I indicated earlier, these refutations concern only the most blatant of
Dr. Jacobsen's assertions.

I must deal more extensively with another gross and intentional distortion
offered by Dr. Jacobsen, and that is the so-called haste and nervous pace with
which the CAD is put together. Here are some facts and figures, not studied
oratory and underhanded insinuations: Since the volumes vary greatly in size
one can state that the entire work will contain 38 units, presented in 20 smaller

or larger individual volumes. Of these, 7 units are either published or in press,
which means that it will take another 20 or even 25 years, to finish the undertaking. If you compare that figure with the _previous_ plan to publish the CAD after 5 years
of further collecting, within a five year period, a plan that was accepted in 1947
by the then director Jacobsen, you will see two things: 1) that Dr. Jacobsen
had very little idea of what the practical problems of the Project were and still
are, and 2) that we are proceeding at a pace that is at least five times slower
than the one he himself envisaged and approved.

What really irks Dr. Jacobsen, I believe, is that work on the Project ~~is~~ _has_ now _bee_
made the main interest of the participants. After so many years of shameful waste
in money, time and working power, editors and staff have come to realize that they
are _engaged in_ ~~working on~~ a living project rather than cynically _making_ ~~deriving~~ a living from it.
Gone are the days when the files were utilized mainly for private special projects -
with the full realization that this meant sabotaging the project. Gone the days
when discussions about varied and abstract scholarly topics were considered more
important than the preparation of reliable and up-to-date information for the files.
What was taken over by Dr. Gelb at the time of his 1947 reorganization was a shocking
accumulation of misinformation (with the exception of the ~~restricted~~ areas where
Dr. Gelb himself had been working). As a result of those conditions (today) we must
spend about 30 percent of our working time merely in checking and correcting what
is in the files. As to the hundreds of words which were misread and hence are not
even there, we have had to make use of my own files which go back some twenty years,
to a time when I never dreamt that I would join the CAD. Evidently Dr. Jacobsen
himself was of the opinion that I was competent enough as a scholar to take charge
of the effort to bring this chaotic agglomeration to life and make it into a dictionary. His support at the outset of my editorship, I may even say his enthusiastic support when, in 1956, I was appointed editor-in-charge in one of the
customary, recurrent crisis situations, is a matter of record. At that time I
made it clear that 1) I consider the Project a finite affair, and 2) that the
work has to be done by a staff genuinely interested in it. Nothing illustrates
better the change in mood and scholarly interest of the staff than the fact that
in these last five years, in which the myth of the perfect file collection and of

the smoothly working organization has been destroyed, more books and articles on assyriological topics were written by the staff than by former collaborators in any corresponding period of time. Which also goes to prove - to ~~whomsoever is~~ anyone open to reason - that the "nervous pace" and terrific pressure exist only in the minds of those who just do not want to face the facts that a) to write a dictionary means to stick out one's neck; b) that there are no "interesting" or "important" words for the lexicographer but just - words; and c) that it is much more difficult to elucidate the meaning of a specific word than to utter trite generalities; in short, that it is much more difficult to work than to lecture one's colleagues.

And that is exactly what Dr. Jacobsen wants, and exactly what I, as the one most responsible for the project, will not stand for. The Project needs more than an absentee-editor who walks in at 5:00 p.m. to dispense two hours of his learning after the staff has been working already for 8 hours, and then complains that his name is not printed prominently enough on the title page. The CAD cannot wait for an editor ~~that~~ who is away for many months on other projects, only to come back and be offended because all work had not stopped in his absence.

This brings me to my final point. Dr. Jacobsen loves to profess - and that at nauseam - that my scholarly thinking is not as deep as his, nor is, for that matter, anybody else's. This, I have found out, means in simple terms that Dr. Jacobsen considers his arguments so wonderful and convincing that he expects all his colleagues to accept them as the only and ~~god-revealed~~ divinely inspired truth. I believe I have shown, however, that no such deep thinking and penetration was in evidence when he concocted his accusations against me.

I have tried hard for years - and these were difficult and nerve-racking years - to get along with Dr. Jacobsen. I have tried to cooperate not only on the CAD but also in the Department, and have encountered nothing but new demands whenever I yielded for the sake of peace. With a consistent policy of persecution, making use of insinuating letters, parliamentary tricks, and ever-changing constitutional amendments, he has attempted to change from being merely one of several members of the editorial board into a kind of Eminence grise, a power in the background, pulling strings. All this, of course, has been promoted under the banner

of "democracy" or "checks and balances," but in fact Dr. Jacobsen uses democratic
phraseology only to obtain hiw own full power just as the Communists do and the
Fascists did before the war in democratic countries.

I am well aware that I have not been the only target of Dr. Jacobsen's zeal
to improve, broaden, deepen and penetrate scholarly thinking. His past record of
resignations speaks for itself, unless one assumes that all the various bodies
with which Dr. Jacobsen found it impossible to cooperate consisted of undemocratic,
incompetent and dishonest individuals. The ideal democratic community of scholars,
in Dr. Jacobsen's mind, seems to be one where a senior member will, when the spirit
moves him, offer his superior wisdom to the junior members for them to accept it with
gratitude and without criticism. Evidently he regards it as inexcusable that I
have, in my tyrannical, undemocratic way, tried to raise the level of cooperation
on the Dictionary Project from one of uninterested subordinate drudgery to one of
enthusiastic devotion, with the full right to questions and criticism recognized
for all participants. I believe that in large measure this has been achieved and
that this spirit of cooperation even has been extended to scholars outside our
Institute. Scholars from many countries are sending us their unpublished material,
and this time without remuneration, in order to advance this great Project.

By way of contrast, you have heard from Dr. Jacobsen himself that he has asked for the
return back "some personal notes, copies of texts and translations of difficult
texts which he had lent to the Dictionary some half year before". I should explain
that the copies mentioned are of texts which the Oriental Institute excavated some
30 years ago and which Dr. Jacobsen has kept outside the Dictionary files ever since.
Apparently this is what he means by "preserving the integrity of his work". Dr.
Jacobsen still has not and probably never will realize that the Project - whenever
he does not interfere - maintains a democratic spirit of intimate collaboration and
mutual respect on the third floor, the working of which he hardly has occasion to
observe on his rare visits. There has never been a time, as long as I have been
Editor in Charge, in which Dr. Gelb or Dr. Landsberger could not tell immediately
which word was being studied and by whom, nor a time in which I have not discussed
freely and informally with these two scholars not only philological questions but every administrative, technical or budgetary problem as well - and discussed these problems

without voting and politicking, as scholars do among fellow scholars whom they respect.

When the Director, Dr. Kraeling, asked me in March, 1959, to stay at the Oriental Institute and with the Dictionary, I declared to him that work on the Project could only go on if the friendly and enthusiastic spirit it had developed and needed for further progress were protected from further willful disruption. This was an important decision that Dr. Kraeling and I had to make - and Dr. Landsberger and Dr. Gelb were fully informed about it. After several months of practically continuous bickering and futile conflict with Dr. Jacobsen we have lived in peace ever since; we intend to continue to do so, in spite of this recent attempt to re-open hostilities.

Nothing can characterize Dr. Jacobsen's mind and its working better than the end-phrase of his statement before the Voting Members, that the Director should be induced "to inquire into possibilities of effectively broadening control with the policies of the Dictionary Project without revoking any firm commitment which he has already made." In other words, after having launched a venomous attack on myself as Editor in Charge, he puts on his alternate mask of sugary reasonableness and wants to be welcomed back into the game again. But the conscious distortion and uncompromising character of the attack itself make it abundantly clear why I cannot even consider such a proposal.

December, 1959   A. L. Oppenheim

KRAELING'S MEMO OF DECEMBER 1959

To the Voting Members of the Oriental Institute:

I have in hand John Wilson's report on your recessed meeting of November 20th and upon the action you took at that occasion. Let me express to all of you my appreciation of your readiness to vote and of the confidence which the vote expressed. We have lived together almost ten years now and I think we ought to understand each other. I am particularly pleased that Thorkild Jacobsen proposed the action taken, because it seems to imply that he has modified the views express in his categorical statement of October 1st, when he declared he had lost all confidence in the Director. It was this statement which, since it was made in public, required that Thorkild have an opportunity to express himself and that you also express your attitude. As for the second part of the action taken, there can be no question about its substance, for we all subscribe to integrity of operation in Institute matters just as we all subscribe to the statement that "the letter killeth but the spirit maketh alive". I appreciate the spirit in which you voted for the motion as a whole, for, as I understand it, nothing in the action was intended to imply that the course of developments leading to the present situation in the administration of the Assyrian Dictionary had in fact stemmed from a neglect or disregard of basic agreements by the Director. This, I take it, was expressed also in your desire to have communications from Leo Oppenheim and myself and in the fact that the meeting was recessed. I take it, therefore, that if after having heard the statements on both sides you were convinced th there had been dereliction of duty on the part of the Director in his relation to the Dictionary project or that the continuance of the present procedure for editing and publishing the Dictionary was not desirable or both, you would so indicate by additional actions, as is your perfect right to do.

I now have in hand also Thorkild's written version of what he said orally at the meeting, which contains serious charges against both Leo and myself. On some of the points at issue Leo can speak more directly than I, on others my testimony is necessary, and I do not hesitate to give it. I will try in my testimony to keep as much as possible to the basic issues, for I have no desire to question the scholarly integrity of anyone including Thorkild. But you will hardly blame me for speaking occasionally with some warmth, because I must say that administratively speaking the Assyrian Dictionary has over the years been the source of more headaches than any other aspect of the life and work of the Institute.

Thorkild's memorandum concerns itself with a concordat adopted in 1954 as a sort of Constitution for the procedure of editing the Assyrian Dictionary. This concordat is the most recent of a series of agreements, understandings, programs, etc., reaching back to 1946 at least. In 1946 there was set down the procedure by which a 2 volume work of 800 pages could be made ready for publication in 1957. In 1950 there was set down an arrangement with the German scholars concerning the von Soden Dictionary. In 1952 a very formal document distributed to Jay as "Editor" and to Benno as "Associate Editor" their respective responsibilities in the pre-paration of the Dictionary articles. Now all of these instruments are good and necessary. I doubt that any of them were ever ratified by the Voting Members and I certainly do not recall that the agreement of 1954 was so ratified or that anybody at that time had the slightest idea that theyshould be so ratified. All I can recall is that I discussed with you as a group or with the Publication Committee or the Policy Committee whether it was correct for the Dictionary group to go ahead and publish without working through the Publication Committee or the Editorial Office. The judgment in that instance was that the Dictionary group should go ahead on its own, first because it had the competence and second because any other course would overburden the Publication Committee and the Editorial Office. The point I am trying to make in this connection is that the Assyrian Dictionary project, group, Board of Editors - call it what you will - has been self-regulating as far as my association with the Institute goes. Its agreements, programs, and understandings are the self-expression of the group adapting itself to changing circumstances. If you the Voting Members were today to be asked to assume a

ratifying or supervisory authority over such agreements, I would urge you by all
means to desist. Judging by past performances you might spend a good deal of
your time doing just that. Besides, the only people who can really resolve the
Assyrianembroglio are the Assyrians themselves, and if not all of them then by
all means those of them who can continue to work together.

Now the fact that the Voting Members have hitherto been spared the necessity
of coping with the Assyrian Dictionary problems does not mean that the Director
is equally so favored. Supervision of the program, the agreements, the progress
and the product as your representative is part of his task and the first thing
I can say on this subject is that your Director has most certainly been involved
in it during the past ten years. After all this is a major enterprise of the
Institute and, whatever its short-comings, it has been receiving and you have been
receiving through it national and international acclaim, now that the volumes have
begun to appear. The Dictionary deserves all the attention the Director can give
it and if I understand the psychology of Thorkild's accusations against Leo and
myself correctly part of what underlies them is the same zeal for the project that
I share with him.

However this may be, the problems of the Dictionary as they have developed
during my ten years as Director have beennumerous and diverse. There are the
problems of differences of judgment on procedure and policy. There are the problems
of staffing and finance, and there are, if we are to be frank, problems of personal
compatibility, of personal habits, of ability to seek and agree to a compromise,
of not holding a decision in the balance forever, which may imply willingness to
admit that someone else may be right and, under certain circumstances, willingness
to make a mistake. What I am trying to say here is that the problems of the
Assyrian Dictionary are continuous and emergent, that they stem outof the reality
of the process of living and of mastering material by the use of the mind, and
that as the problems are emergent so also the solutions are necessarily emergent,
requiring constant adjustments to fit the changing situations.

Now what is it that you the Voting Members can properly expect of your Director
in the discharge of his responsibility for the supervision of such a project as the
Assyrian Dictionary? You can properly expect him to keep the enterprise alive and

moving and to resist the pernicious tendency so well exemplified by Russia at the
UN always to raise the previous question and insist on protocol. This is the surest
wayto kill anything. Les I be misunderstood in this connection I do not by this
mean sacrificing the scholarly merit of the product. This is a prime consideration
for any scholarly institution such as ours, but on this point Leo can have more to
say than I, though I propose to come back to this subject again later. You can
require your Director to let the group regulate its own affairs so far as that is
possible and let its decisions arise from within. On all matters that require his
participation or action you can expect your Director to get the best advice he can
get fromthose in and around the group and to sift it carefully. This I have always
tried to do in consultations with Thorkild, with Benno, with Jay, with Leo and with
Hans Güterbock. I could not possibly have agreed with all of them all the time
but I have never acted contrary to the judgment of all or contrary to the judgment
of Benno. The final thing you can expect of your Director is that when action on
his part is required and when he has clarified his own judgment by consulting those
who have judgment to give, he act promptly, effectively, and as far as possible
inharmony with the earlier developments. This is really all that happened in the
present instance save that the Director had thistime to disagree with Thorkild.

What happened to Thorkild in this connection was only what Jay had gone through
in 1954 when another similar disagreement developed that caused his resignation as
"the Editor" of the Dictionary. At this point I am able to come back to the
"valid agreements" of which Thorkild spoke to you, indicating that with respect
to such I had been derelict in my duty to you. Previously I made the point that
the agreements in question are in essence and must be in practice instruments by
did what Thorkild did, he resigned, only he did not suggest that the Director, who
attended the painful session in which it all happened, had been guilty of it all
and hence derelict in his duty. I mention this not to make a special point of
this fact but because this was the beginning of a series of changed conditions
inside the Dictionary group which bore their full fruitage in 1958-59. Jay was
deeply hurt and refused to paeticipate actively in the work on the first volume
of the Dictionary now put in the hands of Leo. I discussed policy in this matter
with Leo and all concerned and our decision was to try to let time heal the wounds.

It did take time but Jay, I am happy to say, did make the adjustment and at a
certain time, I don't know exactly when, Leo reported to me that Jay was happy and
willing to be consulted on points of grammar, where he has special competence,
and that his help was being asked for and was appreciated. But the basic fact is
did what Thorkild did, he resigned, only he did not suggest that the Director, who
attended the painful session in which it all happened, had been guilty of it all
and hence derelict in his duty. I mention this not to make a special point of
this fact but because this was the beginning of a series of changed conditions
inside the Dictionary group which bore their full fruitage in 1958-59. Jay was
deeply hurt and refused to paeticipate actively in the work on the first volume
of the Dictionary now put in the hands of Leo. I discussed policy in this matter
with Leo and all concerned and our decision was to try to let time heal the wounds.
It did take time but Jay, I am happy to say, did make the adjustment and at a
certain time, I don't know exactly when, Leo reported to me that Jay was happy and
willing to be consulted on points of grammar, where he has special competence,
and that his help was being asked for and was appreciated. But the basic fact is
that Jay disappeared from the active workers on the Dictionary - remaining "an
editor" in name but functioning only in a consultative capacity. Indeed Jay has
told me himself that he could not possibly edit articles prepared by the junior
staff members for the Dictionary because his approach was so different from that
authorized in the 1954 change-over that he would have to do them all over again.
However this may be, the Board by virtue of its own internal developments, had
lost one effective person.

I promised not to dwell on inconsequential matters contained in Thorkild's
statement but there is one that I cannot pass over. This is the one about the
horn-tooting parade that Margy Bell organized when the first volume of the Dictionary
went to press, in her typical refusal to be overawed by professional solemnity.
Thorkild makes this the occasion for one of his barbed comments that the one thing
the overjoyed Director neglected to do was to get the consent of the Editors.
This is just contrary to fact, for the letters which I sent to the editors soli-
citing their imprimatur on form and substance on August 3, 1955 are on file in
the office here and so is my "go-ahead" to Leo based on four "yes" on from and

three on substance. The file includes the ballots cast including Thorkild's "yes
on both counts". But to rpoceed.

The next development inside the Board was Thorkild's non-availability and a
growing deterioration of personal relations with Leo who was working hard to keep
the wheels turning. This matter Leo can tell you more about if he wishes to do so.
I was watching the phenomenon and recall that whenever the matter of Thorkild's
taking on other commitments came up I queried him about their effect upon his
Dictionary work. He was always optimistic - overly so, I fear, - but I did not
feel I should interfere since in my judgment this was something for Thorkild to
work out inside the framework of the Dictionary group. What made the situation
perilous was the special prerogatives Thorkild had obtained as sole arbiter of what
was said in the Dictionary on matters Sumerian. A serious lag in the arrival of
this material could very well drive an "editor in charge" to despair. Something
like this seems to have happened in connection with Thorkild's Diyala enterprise,
from which time the estrangement between Thorkild and Leo became more marked and
as the result of which the effective editorial staff was reduced to Benno, Leo and -
in a junior capacity - of Erica. Should I have repoeted to you that "valid agreements" were being disregarded? I realized that changes were going on, but I felt
the matter was an intra-Dictionary affair, and that with Benno and Leo and Erica
working hard things would work themselves out. Besides, I knew and understood how
difficult were the circumstances under which Thorkild was working, circumstances
that would have led anyone less devoted to waive his prerogatives and to reduce
his commitments.

On the unfortunate events of 1958-59 as I lived through them I shall try to
be more brief even at the risk of seeming to leave unanswered charges of table-
pounding. We all of us deplore that matters of principle have to be worked out
in the hurly-burly of specific situations, not in cool abstraction, but this is
what life is like as all of us should know. I was scarcely on my feet again after
a summer in the hospital when the first rumblings of the newest crisis were heard
and I made a special trip from the east coast (November, 1958) partly to help
as best I could. The occasion was a memorandum from Thorkild to Leo freighted
with barbs and seeming to imply as did also his statement of November 17th to you

that over against the "great Olympians" editors in charge and directors are chore-

boys. We managed to keep the ship afloat through that episode, but then came the

invitation to Leo to move to Johns Hopkins, an enviable and excellent offer for

him, one that serves to show how much greater was the esteem in which Leo was held

outside of Chicago than by Thorkild, a fact which may have aggravated Thorkild's

disturbed mental state.

As to the developments that followed I can only assure you that:

1) It was at no time a part of the thinking of Leo or myself to abandon

   the collegiate procedure of operation in the preparation and approval

   of the Dictionary volumes or to exclude others than himself from assuming

   top responsibility for individual volumes (see Leo's memorandum to me

   dated March 25, 1959). What was at issue was the kind of working conditions

   that would make it worthwhile for an active editor such as Leo to decide

   to spend the rest of his life working on the Dictionary. What more Leo

   originally asked for was agreement to the continuance of his appointment

   as Editor in charge for one year beyond my retirement as Director.

2) That Thorkild cannot escape from a part at least of the way the situation

   became complicated and aggravated during a series of discussions and

   negotiations subject to a sharp dead-line and dealing with a very concrete

   matter.

3) That when the decision had finally to be reached at a meeting of the Board

   held in the Director's Study, Thorkild found his position not shared by

   Benno.

4) That Thorkild turned over his vote to me without any mention of his

   resigning in case I were to vote with Benno so far as my memory goes.

5) That Benno voted to "give Leo what he asks", that Jay voted no and that

   voting by proxy as a member of the Board I went with Benno. If Thorkild

   says that I "did not bother to take a vote" - this is true only to the

   extent that there was no written ballot. All three of us at the table

   did at my request state their positions in the form of a vote. I drew

   the obvious conclusion and took the necessary administrative steps with

   Leo and Dean Harrison.

6) That what vote approved, what I recommended and what Leo and Harrison
    accepted was the continuance of Leo's appointment as Editor in Charge
    for a period of three years beyond June 30, 1960, and his designation as
    Director of the Assyrian Dictionary Project, which gave him the admini-
    strative competence of a Field Director in making junior appointments
    (see my letter to Leo dated March 11, 1959).

The next day Thorkild resigned. What happened here was again a development
working itself out inside the Dictionary group - leading in this case to the
resignation not of "the Editor", but of "an editor" namely Thorkild. This is
regrettable, but apparently from his point of view unavoidable. I am not conscious
of any animus, but I was under the necessity of bringing about a decision one way
or another. My own judgment as expressed in my vote was based upon conversations
with Benno and Hans as well as upon my knowledge of the situation. The following
things emerged from these conversations and I hope my memory here is accurate.

1. None of the Board Members wanted Jay to resume the editorship of the
    Dictionary, because they did not want the articles written as he had
    insisted they must be written.

2. Benno, Hans and I believed that it was undesirable to turn the editorship
    over to Thorkild. I cannot vouch for the reasons the others had for their
    judgment, but as for myself I felt that his personal situation, his work
    habits, his previous record of obligations voluntarily assumed but re-
    maining incomplete made it unwise for us and unfair of us to impose this
    burden on him.

3. Benno, Hans, Thorkild and I all agreed it would be a waste of Benno's
    particular value to saddle him with the job of editor in charge.

It followed from this that if Leo were to leave that would in effect put an
end to the Dictionary, which was a thing the Institute could not afford. In other
words I think we saved the Dictionary, even if we left Thorkild aggrieved, and
if the others who were involved in the developments will recall them, I think they
will agree that we were greatly relieved.

So far as Thorkild's resignation is concerned I refused to accept it for two

reasons only. The first was that I felt that as the Institute's star Sumerologist
he had a moral obligation to contribute to the Dictionary even if he could not
always have his own way. After all, his special prerogatives remained uncontested.
The second was that, as in the case of Jay, I hoped that time would heal the wounds
and that eventually, like Jay, he would make his adjustment. This hope was blasted
in connection with the final episode of 1958-59 when the tenure appointees among
the Voting Members gathered in this office to consider what to recommend apropos
of the invitation that had come to Erica to accept an appointment at Harvard.
This was the occasion at which Thorkild publicly accused Benno and Hans of having
"rigged" the invitation, because of the way they had replied to an inquiry from Harvard.
Everyone was incensed. My feeling was that Thorkild had effectively cut himself off
from the Dictionary group by this statement. Therefore on the next day I accepted
his resignation from the Board.

Again, as I see it, something from inside the Board itself - in this instance
a frantic search for some means of self-justification - had necessarily to lead to
a loss for the Board. I am much more regretful of the mental anguish that caused
Thorkild by his extreme statement to cut himself off from the group and more regretful
of the necessity of rehearsing all this, than I am of his having now shifted his
animosity to me and having charged me with dereliction of duty.

As for the questions about production tempo and scholarly excellence in
Dictionary production, Leo can speak more effectively than I, for which reason I
add only two observations. The first is that there must always be a fine balance
between the two, but that Leo and Thorkild have each only ten years to go before
retirement and that ten years is not too much for the work to be completed in
their terms of service as it should. My second observation is that Leo and I
have long since discussed such matters as maintaining the highest possible standards
and are leaving no stone unturned in the effort to uphold them. The problem here
is in part at least financial - for the more scholars cut themselves off from
service to the Dictionary, for reasons of their own, the more difficult it is to
find replacements for them as workers. In this connection I will gladly state
that it will be my policy so long as I am Director of the Institute to give the
fullest support and high praise to Benno and Leo and Erica and Jay as the ones who

are carrying the Dictionary burden and in and through whom the agreements and
conventions of the past are working themselves out in accordance with the changing
circumstances.

Whether, having heard both Leo and myself, you will wish to hear rebuttals from
Thorkild and re-rebuttals from Leo and me, and whether you will wish to take new
actions that would imply my factual dereliction of duty and thus change the intent
and meaning of the action you took on November 20th, I leave entirely to you. I
personally do not wish to prolong the controversy, partly because I think it will
serve no purpose but mainly because I wish above all that Thorkild may find that
peace with himself that he so richly deserves. I doubt if he will find it along
the line he is following, but I have confidence that given time he will find it.
Because I believe it would be helpful to him and to us all I would therefore move
that we cast one rising vote of such confidence in Thorkild Jacobsen, personally
and as a Sumerologist, and that the meeting be declared adjourned therewith.

LANDSBERGER'S ASSESSMENT OF JANUARY 1961

Abstract of Landsberger's Paper
submitted to John Wilson
on Jan. 25, 1961

After a detailed study of Jacobsen's valuable "Spot-Check of CAD vol. 7", I presented two papers to Dr. Wilson; one contains my critical evaluation of Jacobsen's paper, the other my opinion of the quality, value, and future of the CAD.

It is not my intention to negate the shortcomings of the CAD; part is due to the general style and philosophy of the Editor-in-Chief; part results from the fact that the CAD must offer provisional interpretations and renderings in anticipation of words and problems to be studied for future volumes; but the reason for the greater part lies in the speed and nervous strain under which the volumes are written. But, regardless of these faults, never could I justifiably condemn to death the entire CAD project. With conviction I adhere to the judgement of von Soden in his 1960 OLZ review that we owe to the editors the utmost of admiration and thanks. Any policy that would depose them, or that would place them under constant surveillance prohibiting freedom of activity, I strongly oppose for its destructiveness. Such an action would deprive Assyriology, and especially its younger generation, of an essential and most usseful handbook. To such an end I, at least, cannot be responsible.

Benno Landsberger
26 Jan. 1961

An Opinion of Quality, Value, and the Future

of the C A D

submitted on Jan. 25, 1961, to Prof. John Wilson, Director of
the Oriental Institute, in reply to T. Jacobsen's (typewritten)
paper entitled 'Spot-Check on the CAD vol.7'
by B. Landsberger

(1)   Shortly before Christmas of 1960 the ~~prping~~of~~.~~ ~~this~~ ~~paper~~ was

entrusted to me by the Director. I spent more than two weeks studying

its fifteen and one-half pages of criticism. As a member of the CAD

staff I would like to thank Prof. Jacobsen for his continuing interest

in this project, and for the factual improvements brought about by his

keen judgements. I express again my regrets that he has left us. But

since this is a fact for which, at the moment, no remedy seems available,

I would like to ask him to publish his paper. Thus, if he wishes to bring

the case of the CAD into the open, he may use my 'defense' of the CAD in

so doing, and may reply to it.

In using the word 'defense' I do not mean that I am trying to cover

up, veil, or minimize those points branded by J. or other critics as

mistakes and considered indicative for the standard of the entire enter-

prise, for I am and have been as sharply critical as anyone about the

individual and the general shortcomings of the CAD; I have shown this on

many occasions in my recent publications by pointing up and nailing down

misunderstood passages. Nor does it make a difference to me whether the

blunders go back ultimately to the original drafter (Prof. Moran of Rome

for the volume under discussion), to me, or to the two acting editors (the

personal responsible can easily be found out by checking the manuscripts).

But, on the other hand, I am not willing to be tolerant of a malevolent

attitude on the part of a critic who sees only the bad side, who generalizes

from individual errors, who exaggerates trifles by turning them into crimes,

and who is blind to the achievements.

(2)   My own check of J.'s 'Spot-check' yielded the following results:

9 cases where criticism is not justified;

6 cases of incorrectness that result from the peculiar translation style;

13 cases of inexactness and sloppiness, for the most part immediately

correctable, even for a beginner;

5 cases of serious and unpardonable blunders, 4 of which are found in

    bilingual passages;

5 cases of 'advanced knowledge', i.e., wherein CAD has reproduced only

    'common' Assyriological knowledge, but J.'s criticism has led to

    new results.

    The five categories listed above have been marked as $\theta, \delta, \beta, \gamma, \delta$

respectively on the margin of my accompanying Ms.

(3)   J.'s criticism coincided roughly with von Soden's review of CAD volumes

E and D (in OLZ 1960:485-489. von Soden confirms J.'s opinion by writing(487):

    "Auf grammatisch einwandfreie Lesungen und Übersetzungen sollte

    noch mehr geachtet werden. .... Elementare Fehler müssten bei der

    Kontrolle des Manuskripts eliminiert werden, auch wenn ihre Zahl

    nicht sehr gross ist." [Italics my own.]

There follows an enumeration of six 'elementary mistakes'; in one case

von Soden is wrong, and three others are problematic.

    In the long list of errors (which, by implication, are not elementary) of

the CAD that he presents, some are mistakes on von Soden's part, some are

problematic proposals, and some are 'emendations' not confirmed by collation.

But, for the greater part, his criticism is justified.

    Despite all this, von Soden writes:

    "Auch hier muss der Dank für die ungeheure Arbeitsleistung der Heraus-

    geber und die Bewunderung für das was trotz der von Aussenstehenden

    gar nicht sachgemäss zu würdigenden Schwierigkeiten erreicht

    worden ist, als erstes zum Ausdruck gebracht werden. ....

    schon jetzt ist eine ganz neue Grundlage für die assyriolo-

    gische Arbeit geschaffen worden .... Die Zahl der berichtigten

    Lesungen und Übersetzungen zu veralteten oder sonst mit mehr

    oder weniger Mängeln behafteten Texteditionen ist gewaltig

    gross und sollte von allen, die sich mit bestimmten Textgruppen

    befassen, gebührend beachtet werden!"

Translated:

    "Here again, the thanks for the gigantic achievement of the work of the editors and the admiration for what has been attained (despite

the difficulties which cannot even be evaluated in an objective way

by anyone who is not familiar with the subject) must first be ex-

pressed.... Even now, there is a completely new basis created for

Assyriological research... The number of corrections in readings

and translations of antiquated or faulty editions of texts is huge,

and everyone who deals with any particular groups of texts should

give thorough consideration to these efforts."

On p. 488 von Soden calls the CAD "ein so neues und durchaus gutes Wörterbuch".

(4)   The feeling of 'gratitude' and 'admiration' as expressed by a Number

one Assyriologist is shared by all the minor stars; I am in possession of

two unprovoked judgements: A. Sachs: "The two dictionaries open a new era

for Assyriology"; F.R.Kraus: "Manna from Heaven!" And indeed, the students

anxiously await each new volume. If I should see real danger for the CAD,

I could collect in one week a unanimous Assyriological request that the work

not be discontinued, that they not be deprived the 'manna from heaven'; at the

same time, perhaps none would hesitate to offer some criticism.

(5)   Another danger that I can envisage is that the two acting editors,

or one of them, would lose that tremendous stamina ~~and patience~~ that has

produced up to now 1600 pages, that patience necessary for working with

thousands of cards overfull with elementary mistakes, and, for the most

part, with inferior helpers. I must repeat what von Soden said: "Anyone

not familiar with all sides of Assyriology and all aspects of this specific

work cannot even imagine what it means to push such a dictionary through

all its stages. Of course, noone who has devoted his whole life to a cause

likes to be charged with elementary mistakes or with incurable sloppiness.

So, von Soden's criticism and the news of J.'s new attack (though I kept

his Ms. quite secret, they could not help seeing me work on something the

contents of which they easily guessed) has had a rather serious depressing

effect, especially on L.O. But, more than this, the suspicion that, after

only one year of relative peace, a new storm gathers on the horizon, that

the person they see as an permanent enemy pulls the strings for behind-the-scene plays

against them -- all this cuts their elan to the quick and slackens their
pace. Already they have interrupted work on the current Sade-volume. They
"threaten" resignation so that they can instead concentrate on their real
vocations, viz. L.O.'s cultural history and E.R.'s descriptive grammar.

Even in the event that the CAD's ship of state could pass safely between
Scylla and Charybdis, it must be admitted that the two acting editors are
overburdened and that the work they do accomplish is done under nervous strain.
They constantly and vainly seek for real help, but it comes to a temporary
nothing; for what rare person, even with limited experience in Assyriology,
would wittingly place himself under this kind of slavery, not preferring an
academic position with moderate teaching and free time for research?

If, and it is my hope, they will continue, certainly they will
not submit to a governess, nor to a periodic 'senate-hearing' wherein
they would have to defend their activities. What I have said in this
section implies, of course, a replacement. There is none, even if five
or six scholars (who do not exist) should be hired.

(6)   One (and perhaps the only) good effect that this new 'crisis' has
                                    (as far as it runs parallel to CAD)
had is that E.R. turned the tables by searching through von Soden's AHw
for mistakes. The crop was considerable; though von Soden tends not to
make elementary mistakes, E.R. was able to find a surprising amount of
sloppiness, arbitrary emendations or separation of items, not to speak of
the well known clumsiness of approach documented at every step by this
great scholar to whom perhaps Assyriology is more indebted than to anyone.
The study by E.R. will appear in Orientalia.

(7)   My 'defense' is not meant to give the impression that I still do not
dream of a CAD that would be so thorough as to render it invulnerable to
the 'superior' rebukes of von Soden and the sarcastic diatribe of Jacobsen
(within the limits, of course, of human error). A definite and essential
improvement will be brought about, a normal developement presupposed,
in that the CAD, after S[1], will work (to put it tersely) on von Soden

[1] Note: Nearly two-thirds of this volume are finished; some years of work
by the drafters (Drs. Kienast and Sweet) and editors are invested; they should
under all circumstances be allowed and also willing to issue this volume. Other
'stock-piles': letter B, draft completed by Dr. Rowton in consultation with the
editors; part os letter S also drafted by Rowton.

and not _for_ von Soden; this means that it will not just pave the way for him
but profit from his work, including the grammatical contributions implicit
in the articles. The firstpreparatory work on the A volume has been done
with a very able and thorough drafter, Dr. Hirsch (former assistant of von Soden
and with Dr. Leichty, under the complete supervision of E.R. and L.O. The
results are encouraging. That certain benefits will have been derived from the
AHw Vorlage, and that it (CAD A) will in some respects have about it
a character of gleaning, is not denied, but any assumption that there
is little left to contribute is quite wrong. Those aspects admittedly
neglected by von Soden (Orientalia 28:26ff.) will be stressed. Not only
because of far richer documentation (especially by collecting the logographic
writings almost completely missing in AHw), but also because of many other
virtues will the CAD stand out over its predecessor. One has only to look
at the rather poor article awīlu "man" in AHw to foresee the task of CAD.
The general impression that von Soden's work makes is that, despite the
gratefulness and admiration we owe him, he has slacked down considerably in
comparison with the standard of his 104 Orientalia contributions. He takes
no pains to penetrate, or to reconcile disparate meanings. He copies CAD
uncritically, and uses Arabic etymologies, a habit known to be detrimental
for a long time. On the whole, the CAD has a greater claim to be called a real
real product of lexicography than does AHw. Though this statement is, in this
context, pretentious, I am going to prove it soon by real 'spot-checks,
dealing with central problems rather than individual passages.

Other improvements may be foreseen if the editors remain in-charge and
if one looks optimistically at the project: a specialist for Sumerian (re-
placing J.) may be employed for improving on the so-called prehistory of the
words; whole sets of cards, e.g., New or Old Assyrian letters, should be
replaced with new ones; the lexical series edited; many other deficiencies
uprooted; and—most desirable—a periodical founded for new source material
and researches (reflections about the establishing of meanings are now
condemned to laconic remarks at the end of individual articles in the CAD).

(8)   It is utopian to think that the CAD can be continued without L.O. and E.R.

(9)   It is the right of the Director of the Oriental Institute or even
the Chancellor of the University to be informed about any achievements,
to have a means of checking, to be asked for counsel if major decisions lay
ahead or if difficulties arise. But the first prerequisite for a successful
relationship of this kind is mutual trust and confidence which belie
suspicion, and such has not been emphasized heretofor.

(10)   A personal remark: I am deeply indebted to the CAD because it has
been the vehicle enabling thousands of details and also essential viewpoints of mine to reach the public, points which otherwise would have
been relegated to oblivion. The fairness of the acting editors in handling
this material must be stressed.

OPPENHEIM'S LETTER TO WILSON, JANUARY 28, 1961

January 28, 1961

John A. Wilson, Director

A. Leo Oppenheim

Assyrian Dictionary

Oriental Institute

Assyrian Dictionary Project

Dear John:

In the course of our discussions I have come to realize that the presentation of my case will not be found in the dossier of the CAD, while those of the other parties concerned will be there in writing. For this reason I would like herewith to state my case for the benefit of any future editor of the CAD and for the benefit of any future director of the Oriental Institute.

In November, 1954, I took over a thoroughly wrecked and demoralized Project with the aim of proving to the Director, to the staff and to the Assyriologists that a dictionary could be put together from the extant files and from what the editors could contribute through their experience, their notes, etc. In the beginning I could rely on Professor Landsberger and Erica Reiner and also, to a limited extent, on Dr. Jacobsen, who established a pattern of personal collaboration with Landsberger and looked over the MS. to contribute suggestions and at times add Sum. material. Since it was not my intention to stop after having brought out one single volume as proof that this could be done, but to continue the project and to strive for the goal of bringing out at least one average size volume per year, I had to continue to work for a time against the opposition of Professor Landsberger and Dr. Jacobsen, both of whom would have preferred to work at their own speed, regardless of the consequences for the Project as such. I did succeed in coming to terms with Professor Landsberger, who realized that he could work only on a certain number of words if the project was to go on, leaving the balance to me and Miss Reiner. This solution has worked out reasonably well ever since, especially since Professor Landsberger has always been extremely cooperative and unstinting with his support and advice. This arrangement has enabled us to bring out volumes at a speed only slightly below the goal set. On the other hand, Dr. Jacobsen did not favor this working method readily but soon began to express his opposition in several ways which need not be discussed here. The tension that developed was increased by his

repeated and lengthy absences from the Institute which I could not allow to interfere
with the work at hand. He objected to what he called the "insane speed," although I
attempted to bring home to everybody concerned that it will take the CAD at least twenty
more years to deal with the entire material—that is, if it is possible to maintain the
staff at the present level, of scholarly competence and psychological interest. In the
year 1958 Dr. Jacobsen began to disrupt the work on the CAD with demands for more and
more meetings, conferences, etc., and to exercise pressure on the members of the staff,
thus impeding progress and undermining morale. Since it became more and more clear to
me that it was not possible to maintain a spirit of cooperation with Dr. Jacobsen, I
was ready not only to leave the project but also the Institute. Director Kraeling succeeded after lengthy and very strenuous discussions, to work out a new modus vivendi for
the project from which Dr. Jacobsen deemed it better to separate himself at that point.
His enmity, personal and against the Project, has still not ceased—but I am not going
into this any further.

Dr. Gelb has cooperated with the CAD ever since 1954, in the way and to the degree
he has established for himself, and has given us material and advice when asked for.

The years since 1954 have been both very hard and very rewarding. Let me speak first
of the rewards. In collaboration with Professor Landsberger and Erica Reiner we have
succeeded in showing new ways and methods in Akkadian lexicography, as has now been
tellingly proven by the Handwörterbuch of von Soden that has put in relief our own contribution. I am very proud to have been working with such a team and with such results.
Miss Reiner and myself have had to work very hard not only to fill the gaps left in the
files but also to incorporate the steady stream of new material that is being published
and has to be transliterated and analysed—ranging from literary and medical to economic
texts. We have succeeded rather well but not as fully as we had intended—all this
work has had to be done in addition to the Dictionary work and beside the personal
scholarly work which the three of us have striven to maintain throughout all these years.

With so few workers, and working at the same time on three distinct levels, a) writing
articles that are too long or too difficult for the junior members of the staff, b) editing and correcting articles for the final manuscript, and c) reading of proofs of the
articles in press, it is inevitable that mistakes have slipped into the finished volumes.
This we knew from the beginning and such mistakes we have been striving to control. The
volumes are getting better in each instance but the very fact that different persons
work on them will always prevent complete uniformity in details, style, etc. We have
been keeping careful track of all errors known to us or made known to us by our Assyriological friends from all over the world, as well as of all additional evidence—pro and
contra—that has been published in the meantime or come to our knowledge. If we had
to choose between perfection without publication and publication with imperfections, we
still today would opt for the latter.

Where do we go from here? We are about to reach a turning point. The pioneer
period will be over with the publication of the Volume Z (in final page proof) and §

(partly finished in final MS). From now on, we will have to take up the letters previously worked out by von Soden's Handwörterbuch, beginning with Volumes A and B. Though
von Soden's treatment of this material will give us some help—especially in providing
references to add to our ever imcomplete files—it will also entail the additional work
of checking on the Handwörterbuch so that one can not predict more than that the present
speed will be maintained. We will not so much need junior staff members as scholars who
can work independently and are able to produce articles that will need only editorial
corrections.

Here is a program as a suggestion and a base for discussion.

I. The editorial board should include the entire permanent team, i. e., Mr. Rowton and
Miss Reiner, who have both been working full time on the project and are naturally
destined to carry on the work. We all can work in mutual trust and reach agreement
in informal talks as we have done all the time. I do not think it is important to
have constitutions or to establish titles, I would rather take up a favorite idea
of Dr. Gelb's and consider us all associates in a common undertaking. The responsibility
budgetwise and towards the Assyriological "world" I shall carry.

II. We desperately need a budget post for a young and interested permanent collaborator
(instructor rank), which should be decently endowed and lead the person eventually
into the fold of the editors. Here I think of Dr. H. H. Hirsch who, in my opinion,
has proven himself not only a serious and diligent worker with an excellent scholarly
training but has also shown that interest in this kind of tedious and difficult work
that we so far have not been able to find in any other of the many young scholars
who have come to us from overseas to participate in the project.

III. We should furthermore have a young man (Ph. D. level) who would stay for a year
or, maximally, two, to help us with filing cards, and with the complex bookkeeping
operation that is constantly going on with new texts, additions, corrections, etc., and
who could learn Assyriology in this way and help us at the same time. The pay should
be modest but decent.

With such a crew—supported by an adequate clerical staff—the CAD may embark on the
long and wearisome "middle passage" that will require even more enthusiasm and, above
all, more stamina than has been needed up to now. It can be reasonably expected to
carry on the work beyond the lifetimes of the "elder" generation of scholars. With
index volumes, and volumes of additions and corrections, my estimate is that it will
take at least twenty years of hard work to produce an opus of which the then director
of the Oriental Institute will have every reason to be proud.

INDEX